Mud wagon, circa 1860.

Pictorial History of California

PICTORIAL HISTORY

OF CALIFORNIA

By Paul C. Johnson

DOUBLEDAY & COMPANY, INC., GARDEN CITY, NEW YORK

A state enriched by three conflicting cultures: Indian, Spanish-Mexican, and Yankee.

Library of Congress Catalog Card Number 72–103759
Copyright © 1970 by Paul C. Johnson
All Rights Reserved
Printed in the United States of America
First Edition

White deer dance, Yurok tribe.

Mission San Carlos Borromeo del Carmelo, 1770.

Yankee gold miners on the Yuba River, 1852.

A golden land, isolated from the world by uncharted seas and a nearly impregnable mountain barricade.

Supply train passing Donner Lake.

Wreck of bark Gifford, *off Lands End.*

Pomp and ceremony marked the end of California's isolation.

Foreword

IF CALIFORNIA were an independent nation today, it would rank first among all the nations of the world in per capita income, second in car ownership, fourth in telephone installations, and seventh in gross production. This astonishing pre-eminence has occurred within a relatively short time as the long span of history goes, and the reasons for this beanstalk growth are manifold.

Much of this development can be attributed to the magnetic pull of the state's natural riches and benign climate that have lured the venturesome from the four corners of the globe. But the unique character of California, the flavor that sets it apart from its forty-nine fellows, is basically derived from the people who have come here to make their way in a land of promise. The story of California is a chronicle of padres stirred by visions of lighting the dark souls of the heathen, of young adventurers called by dreams of gold, of solid citizens and hardened criminals attracted here to earn a living, of settlers and boomers, of farmers and engineers. It is the story of people responding to the challenge of a new environment and laboring to manipulate it to their own ends, for good or ill.

The chronicle of the people who shaped this state is the subject of this book, presented in visual form. Only those events and trends that help to explain California today have been favored for inclusion. Happenings that merely made headlines or reflected trends common to the country as a whole have been generally excluded, for this book is not an almanac.

In assembling the pictures, the author has endeavored to rely on graphic material created during each historical era or on later creations that capture the flavor of earlier times. This task has entailed considerable winnowing, spasms of serendipity, and gracious help from collectors and custodians of pictorial materials. In this project, the author was assisted by several willing hands, duly credited in the acknowledgments in the Appendix. He wishes to acknowledge in particular the help of Robert A. Weinstein, of the Los Angeles County Museum of Natural History, and John Barr Tompkins, of the Bancroft Library, for services beyond the call of duty. Special appreciation must be expressed to Judith Whipple, who designed and laid out this book and generally helped to row it through the editorial shoals, and to Luther Nichols and Sally Arteseros of Doubleday for understanding and forbearance.

If medals are ever minted for author's wives, one should certainly be awarded to my wife, Genie, who patiently endured the role of author's widow during the long months of the book's creation. To her, this book is fondly dedicated.

PAUL C. JOHNSON

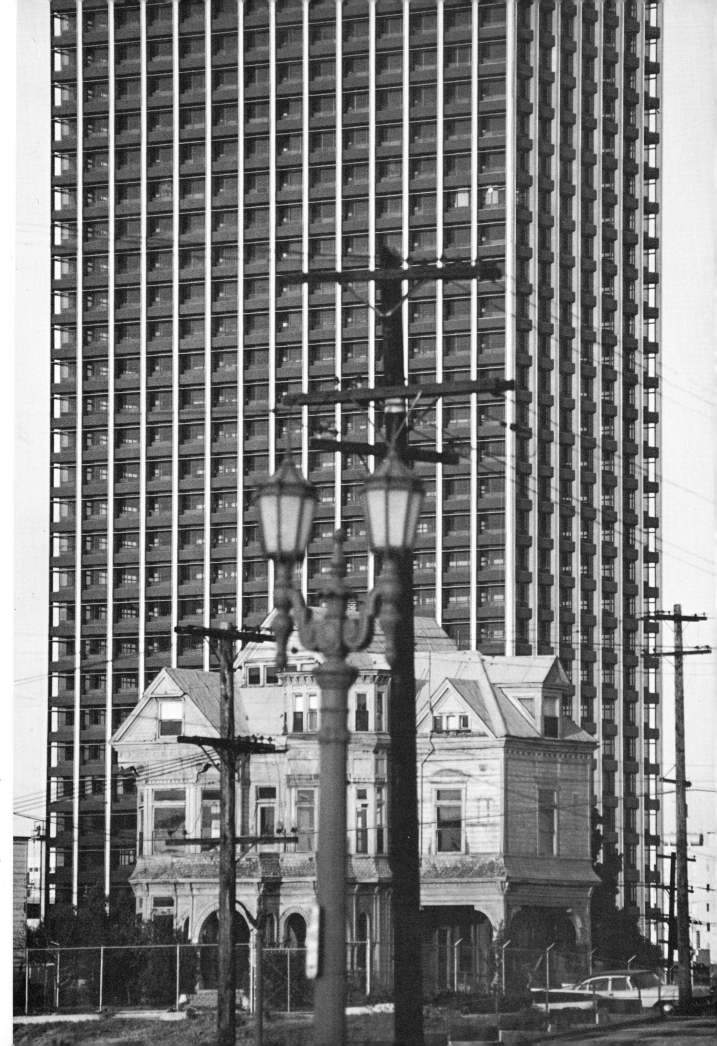

Contents

1542-1769

Legend and Lure

"Know, then, that, on the right hand of the Indies, there is an island called California, very close to the side of the Terrestrial Paradise . . . In the whole island, there is no metal but gold. The most precious stones are to be found like the stones of the field for their abundance."

So reported a widely circulated historical romance of 1510 that went on to relate that the island was "peopled by black women without any men among them, for they lived in the fashion of Amazons. Their arms were of gold, and so was the harness of the wild beasts that they tamed and rode." They were ruled by a Queen Calafiá, who was "very large in person, the most beautiful of them all, of blooming years, strong of limb and of great strength." The women kept their island pure of men with a scavenger corps of griffins that devoured men and boys.

From this beguiling tale, familiar to the Spaniards who conquered Mexico in the 1520's, came the name California, first applied to the Baja Peninsula, which was thought to be an island, and then gradually extended northward to the limits of the Spanish domain in the Pacific Northwest.

It took more than a captivating legend to make the practical-minded Spaniards explore and settle

The first Europeans to set foot on California soil found the Indians friendly and co-operative. When Francis Drake landed in 1579, the natives took him for a great spirit, brought him gifts and necklaces, and crowned him as their chief. He stayed thirty-six days, claimed the region for Queen Elizabeth I.

the new land. Remotest of the remote outposts in Spain's world dominions, California was not considered of value in its own right, but was treated as a steppingstone to somewhere more important and was thus left undisturbed for 250 years after Spain initially claimed it.

At the time of the conquest of Mexico in 1521, Spain and Portugal divided the world between them into two immense empires. An accommodating encyclical of the pope in 1493 allocated all new lands west of the fiftieth meridian to Spain, everything east to Portugal. Actually, neither the governments of Spain and Portugal nor the Papacy had any notion of the enormity of the territories assigned to each. The two empires found themselves in possession of vast territories that expanded as the boundaries of the known world evolved, to the point that they were hard pressed to supply, administer, or defend the half-worlds under their nominal control.

When Cortes landed on the east coast of Mexico in 1519 and marched inland, he was under the delusion that the new country was part of a large island off the coast of China. Europeans at that time still believed that there was only one massive continent in the Northern Hemisphere with Europe along one edge and China on the eastern rim. When Columbus made port in the Caribbean he was certain that he had reached the backside of the Eurasian continent and had found a short cut to the Indian Ocean. Succeeding sea explorations gradually revealed the true lay of the land, but it took fifty years for North America to expose itself as another continent.

From the sixteenth century on, voyagers persisted in a belief that there was a maritime short cut from the Orient to Europe over the top of the world. Known as the Northwest Passage, or the Strait of Anian, as marked on this 1578 map, it was sought by countless expeditions and finally abandoned as a myth. The passage was actually found, however, but not until 1903, when Roald Amundsen sailed through it in the Gjoa (now on display in Golden Gate Park).

Ignorant as they were of world geography, the Spanish were even more in the dark about the unexplored lands that lay to the north and south of Mexico City. But they started out quickly to learn more about the land they owned by papal right.

Insatiably seeking more treasure, the mercenary Spaniards followed every will-o'-the-wisp rumor of gold, gems, and luxuries. Land parties composed of military and priestly elements moved up the ever-broadening waist of Mexico, conquering and establishing missions as they progressed, ultimately penetrating into present-day Kansas and as far as the Great Lakes.

The western borderlands beyond the desert were the last to feel the colonizers' footfall. Demands of the wide territory already subdued absorbed the total energies of the overextended colonial machinery, and there was neither capital nor manpower to divert to unknown lands farther west. Gone were the swashbuckling days of the conquistadors. Un-

less a new land offered prospect of immediate and extensive profits, it was left to look out for itself.

Desultory efforts at colonizing and exploring the Californias had been carried on at scattered intervals. Abortive excursions in quest of immediate gain resulted in the discovery of Baja California in 1532, when Cortes found the lucrative pearl fishery at the tip of the peninsula, but a subsequent colonizing venture there was starved out. Ships sent north along the coast of Mexico proved the existence of the gulf and the long peninsula opposite, but also gave rise to the myth of California as an island. Navigators who sighted the mouth of the Colorado River mistook it for one end of a strait separating an island from the mainland and perpetuated an error that dogged mapmakers for decades.

Land travel to the Californias would have been slow, expensive, and hazardous. Overland caravans required an immense baggage train to make them self-supporting while they crossed untracked terrain and to feed them when they reached their destination. The slow-moving pack trains were vulnerable to Indian attack and were prey to starvation and thirst when their stock ran out of water or feed.

Travel by sea was just as perilous and had some special hazards of its own. Crammed into small, poorly equipped vessels, unreliable crews of impressed seamen and untrained natives had to suffer from exposure to wind and wave, heat and cold, inedible food, and the scourge of scurvy.

Furthermore, the science of navigation was still so primitive that captains made prodigious miscalculations that sent them hundreds of leagues off course. Sea charts were unreliable and sprinkled with blanks which concealed shoals and treacherous currents.

In the Spanish lexicon, New Spain's northwestern land mass ranked low in the value scale. Assumed to be deficient in precious metals, cities of gold, and other compelling mirages of the day, it offered nothing that could compete with the overwhelming treasure troves at opposite ends of Spain's half-world in Latin America and the West Indies.

New Spain became a way station in the movement of luxury goods to the home country. Treasure ships from all parts of the New World unloaded their cargoes in Mexican ports for transshipment to Spain. And after an ocean connection with the Orient was established in 1565, the valuable cargoes from the Indies, once carried thousands of miles overland by caravans, were sailed across the Pacific to New Spain for reshipment to Madrid.

Authorities in New Spain looked for new ways to protect the long runs of the treasure galleons from the Indies and to shorten the distance between the Orient and Spain itself. Here is where California finally acquired momentary importance. Voyagers were ordered to explore the west coast and find, if possible, a short cut over the roof of the world to Spain. Secondly, they were commissioned to chart the shoreline and find suitable harbors where the treasure vessels could anchor after five months at sea and make repairs, replenish supplies, and rest the exhausted passengers and crew. This innocent objective took on a more menacing importance after 1548, when privateers began to find the fat Spanish treasure ships. A haven along the California shore seemed all the more important after 1579, when a master privateer, Francis Drake, had the audacity to land in California itself, remain

there six weeks, and claim the whole territory for England. Other British sea dogs followed his trail, and they in turn were followed by buccaneers from Holland and France, forcing the Spaniards to defer some of their expansionist activities until they could strengthen their naval defenses.

So it was that the first Spanish subjects to set foot on the soil of what was later to become Alta California were engaged in surveys to determine the feasibility of using the land as a defense bastion or a stop on the way to a more important place. Their findings reassured the authorities in New Spain that California was well worth holding for possible future development but not worth the expense of crash colonization.

The Spanish explorers discovered two good ports, the sheltered bay of San Diego and the open crescent at Monterey, but they sailed right past the narrow slot leading to the magnificent harbor of San Francisco. Had they discovered it in the early years of exploration, it is reasonable to assume that Spain would have taken immediate steps to colonize California—an action that would have changed the course of Western history. A flourishing colony established here in the sixteenth century might have become so firmly rooted that it would have been impossible to dislodge, and would conceivably still be a part of Mexico today.

In the meantime, it was Monterey that held the limelight during the century and a half of neglect. Its harbor had been so lavishly praised by its discoverer in 1602 that it held a key position in Spain's plans for the eventual settlement of California, which called for developing the port and establishing the provincial capital there.

California slumbered on, visited by an occasional galleon in distress, but mainly left to itself. This tranquil state could not last indefinitely, and it was finally dispelled by aggression from an unexpected quarter. Hitherto concerned about her archenemy England, with whom she had been at war off and on for decades, Spain suddenly found herself confronted by Russia, which had expanded eastward to the Pacific Ocean and was moving even farther eastward, impelled by the lure of sea otter pelts, toward Spain's northwestern borderlands.

California was no longer to be left alone—nor were the natives, whose Arcadian existence was soon to be crushed under Spanish domination.

Of Pearls and Amazons

Ever seeking treasure, the hardheaded Spaniards were surprisingly susceptible to rumors and legends. Once they had reached the Pacific, they turned north and south seeking new booty, drawn by tales of golden cities, islands of pearls, and precious stones in abundance. Always just beyond the reach of each returned explorer lay the treasured land, ready to empty its cornucopia on the next man to try for it.

The land to the north was an absolute blank. In the absence of exact information, the Spanish relied on myths and legends extracted from the natives and occasional travelers who claimed to have visited the Terrestrial Paradise to the north. Thus it was that the first approaches to California were frosted over with legend and tall tales.

Most durable of legends, the notion that California was an island persisted for two hundred years. The error was launched in the 1500's by explorers who mistook the mouth of the Colorado for the end of a strait. Though disproved by explorations of Father Kino in 1701, the myth was rekindled from time to time, even by the Spaniards after they knew better. European mapmakers perpetuated the error as late as 1748, just twenty years before Spanish colonists founded a settlement in San Diego.

Restless Cortes, not content with the fabulous treasures of Mexico, discovered a rich pearl fishery at the tip of the Baja peninsula in 1534 and there founded the first—if short-lived—settlement in California. Pearls, harvested two hundred feet down by divers, netted immense profits—as much as 4500 per cent!

Secret weapons of Calafía, mythical warrior queen of the Island of California, were said to be griffins (half eagle, half lion) that were trained to eat men. Released in a major battle, the beasts caused a humiliating defeat by devouring the queen's allies along with the enemy.

Voyagers' Fateful Gamble

When the first explorers sailed from New Spain to survey the coast of California, they set forth on a perilous and tedious adventure. In ships that were small, leaky, and clumsy they packed a crew often of scoundrels, navigated with unreliable instruments that provided only half the information they needed and sometimes led them far off course, subsisted on monotonous and verminous food, and, after several months at sea, coped with the dreaded scurvy that killed 40 to 75 per cent of the crew on long voyages.

The coastwise explorers kept within sight of land, unless blown out to sea by storms, and tacked their way north against prevailing winds. On such voyages, the pilot was more important than the captain, for on him devolved the responsibility for reconnoitering uncharted harbors and rocky shores and selecting safe anchorages and landings. An error in pilot judgment could wreck a ship; the loss of a pilot could blind a vessel, force it to limp home.

Marine navigation in the sixteenth century, though advancing rapidly, was still part necromancy. Printed charts, which first began to appear in the sixteenth century, were prepared with treacherous blanks in information, filled in with drawings of sea monsters, vessels under full sail, or elaborate compass roses. The drawing at the right, reproduced from the cover of a seventeenth century marine atlas, shows geographers surrounded with the imperfect tools of their trade, hovered over by denizens of the zodiac and flights of reassuring cherubim.

La Nueva y Grande Relumbrante
ANTORCHA DE LA MAR,
QUE CONTIENE
La description de las coftas Maritimas Meredionales de la *Mar* del *Nord*, de la Mancha, Inglaterra, Efcocia

Cartoon by Holbein captures the unhappy mood of sixteenth-century sailors, bolstering their courage as they stand off to sea. Long voyages were hazardous, usually fatal ventures for seamen, and crews sometimes had to be dragged from prisons. If a ship returned at all, it was liable to bring back fewer than half the men who shipped out on her, the rest lost to accidents, fights, or scurvy. The vessels were small, cramped for space, not much larger than present-day harbor tugs and with passenger space less than that in a Greyhound bus.

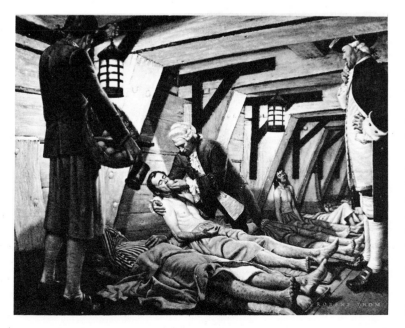

Dr. James Lind, administering a lemon to a victim of scurvy, is credited with discovering the cure for this traditional seamen's death. Caused by dietary deficiencies on long voyages, the disease set in after four months at sea, rapidly killed the afflicted unless copious intake of antiscorbutics could be induced. Most reliable cures: citrus, potatoes, onions, or green vegetables.

Highly romanticized interpretation of Juan Cabrillo's landing at Ventura in 1542 adorns the Santa Barbara County Courthouse. Cabrillo named the site El Pueblo de las Canoas for the remarkable Chumash canoes that swept out to meet his vessels. Honored as California's Columbus, Cabrillo is memorialized by dozens of statues and plaques, a bridge, several parks, schools and boulevards, a marine museum, a national historical monument, and an annual music festival.

Discovery and Rediscovery

Discovery of California is officially credited to Juan Rodríguez Cabrillo, the first European to set foot on the shore of what has since become the state. Under instruction to find a passage from the Pacific to the Atlantic oceans, he sailed north along the coast in 1542, visiting the Indians, mapping the shoreline, and christening every landmark in sight. His flotilla sailed as far north as the Rogue River, where the ships were driven back by storms. Cabrillo died on the voyage and was buried on San Miguel Island.

Following in his wake sixty years later, a wily merchant named Sebastián Vizcaíno sailed north to find a site for a colony, blithely renaming all the landmarks that Cabrillo had previously christened. He found his ideal location at Monterey and requested permission to found a colony there. It was granted, then refused by a new viceroy who rejected the site as too exposed to foreign seizure, too remote to supply and defend.

(left) 1542 Cabrillo's flagship, San Salvador; *lateen-rigged, one hundred tons' burden, about seventy-five-foot length. (right) 1602, Vizcaíno's flagship,* San Diego; *square-rigged, two hundred tons' burden, about eighty-foot length.*

"It is the best port that could be desired for commodiousness, and is sheltered from all the winds." So wrote Sebastián Vizcaíno in 1602, describing the exposed crescent of Monterey Bay. This exaggerated picture gained him authorization to plant a colony there, but he was double-crossed and sent to Japan instead, and the port was unvisited for 167 years.

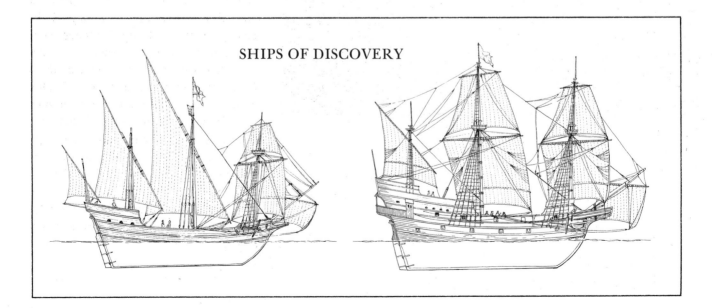

SHIPS OF DISCOVERY

Irresistible targets for freebooters, the Manila galleons were never safe from attack, and several were seized by British ships. Here, H.M.S. Centurian *captures the galleon for 1743 in Philippine waters after a brief and bloody battle. The British captain outgunned the Spanish vessel and made off with eight million dollars in booty.*

Haven for Treasure Ships

Once a year for two and a half centuries following 1565, a treasure-laden galleon sailed east from Manila to New Spain in what was described as the "longest and most dreadful voyage of any in the world."

Vessels left Manila in June to avoid the fearsome Pacific storms, but still suffered weeks of gales, fog, and cold. The trip took seven months, five on the open sea. The storm-tossed vessels made a landfall near Monterey or Baja California, but never dropped anchor. Galleon captains were too eager to reach Acapulco, where fortune awaited them, to stop once they had sighted land. One attempt was made to find a suitable port in California, where ships could flee from privateers, repair storm damage, or recuperate ailing crews, but the survey ended in disaster and no further tries were made to locate a haven. After 1775, the galleons were required to stop at Monterey, but, as far as can be ascertained, few did.

Marine chart of 1581 shows circular route of Manila galleons. Eastbound ships followed Japan Current on seven-month voyage. Return across southern latitudes took only two months. Note that this chart correctly shows California as part of mainland rather than an island. The island myth did not appear on maps until well into the next century.

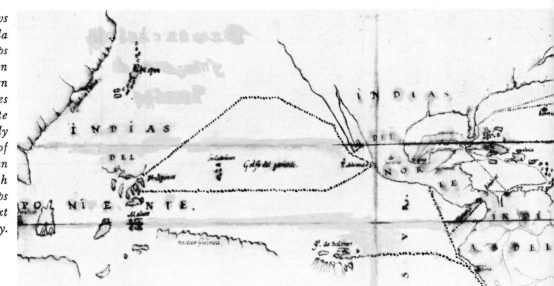

Cargo valued at millions of dollars made the solo voyages at immense profit. Legal limit was 100-per-cent gain, but shipments usually brought two to three times more, due to loopholes in the law. Cargo space was sold to merchants and they were free to stow as much treasure as they could into the allotted space. Even crewmen were permitted to buy space and some of them made fortunes.

Shards of chinaware shattered on the beach of Drakes Bay in 1595, are still being found nearby. Chests of china, packed in loose clay, were part of priceless cargo of galleon under Cermeño driven ashore while engaged in survey for a suitable port in California. Typical cargo: sandalwood, silks, spices, gum, edible birds' nests, quicksilver, tea.

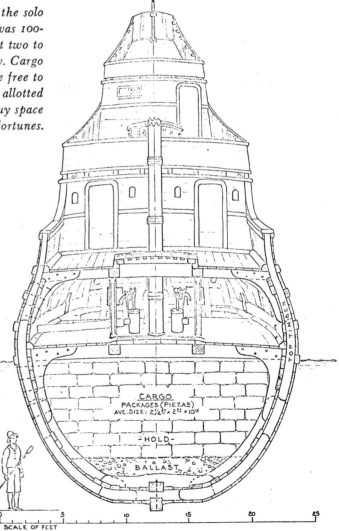

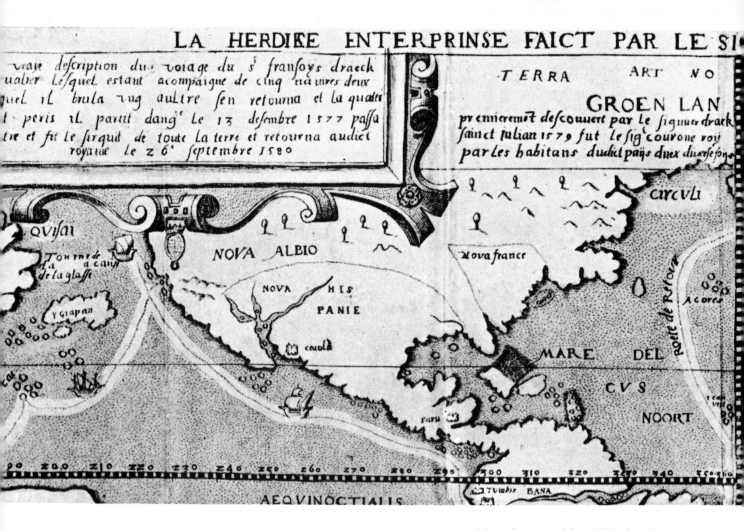

vraje defcription du voiage du s' franfoys draech
ualier lefquel estant acompaigne de cinq navures deux
quel il brula vng aultre fen retourna et la quatri
t peris il partit dang' le 13 defembre 1577 paffa
tre et fit le firquit de toute la terre et retourna audict
royaue le 26 septembre 1580

TERRA   ART   NO

GROEN LAN
premieremt defcouuert par le figuur drack
sainct Julian 1579 fut le fig courone roij
par les habitans dudict pays duex duerse fur

QVISAI

NOVA ALBIO

nova france

NOVA HIS PANIE

CIRCVLI

Acores

MARE   DEL

CVS

NOORT

AEQVINOCTIALIS

The First New England

Forty years before the English set foot on Plymouth Rock, Francis Drake landed in California and claimed it for Queen Elizabeth under the name Nova Albion—New England.

His mission was to harass Spanish settlements along the eastern rim of the Pacific—an assignment he fulfilled with gusto, sacking towns, taking ships, and seizing booty as he sailed north from Cape Horn. His stay in California convinced him that the area would make an ideal locale for an English base, and after he returned home in 1580, he recommended its occupation. According to one authority, he was actually authorized to pursue such a venture, but his colonizing fleet was betrayed and captured by the Spaniards.

Drake's entry into Spain's private lake, the Pacific, galvanized the Spaniards into taking corrective measures. It also encouraged buccaneers to prey on Spanish ships, and it gave England a claim on the land.

Map of the world published in France in 1581 after Drake's return showed New England stretching eastward all the way to the French colonies on the East Coast. Drake sailed around world in 1577–80, was knighted 1580, was vice-admiral of fleet that defeated Armada in 1588.

Leaking from a year's voyaging, Drake's vessel, the Golden Hind, was careened in shallow water at Drakes Bay by gingerly shifting heavy cargo of booty to her port side. Crew spent six weeks repairing and calking seams. The party built a stone fort on the beach as protection against Indians, who proved unexpectedly friendly. Exact site of Drake's landing (right) has been a matter of debate among historians, but is now acknowledged as the bay that bears his name. Significant piece of evidence is this small map, inset in a map of the world by Hondius (1588), which correlates exactly with modern charts of Drakes Bay.

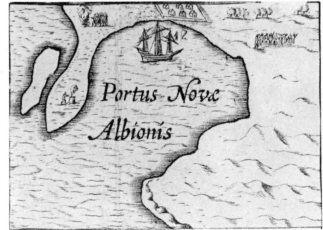

When the party left, Drake "set up a monument of our being there, and also of her Majesties right and title to the same, namely a plate, nailed upon a faire great poste." Three hundred years later, the plate was found by a chauffeur waiting for his employer to return to the car. Metallurgists and historians examined it for two years and certified it genuine.

Threat from the North

Alarming news of a Russian invasion of New Spain's northwestern frontier began to filter to Madrid in the 1760's. Jarred out of its lethargy, the Spanish government ordered the immediate occupation of California to block the southward expansion by the interlopers. In addition, the viceroy dispatched a squadron north as far as Alaska to formally repossess the land.

The Russians were well established as a power in the North Pacific. Since the 1740's, a lucrative trade in sea otter pelts had progressively advanced the Russians eastward along the Aleutian chain toward the mainland and had caused the building of bases in what is now Alaska.

The valuable furs soon attracted traders from other nations. The English sea captain James Cook, in search of the Northwest Passage, stopped in Nootka Sound in 1778 and purchased a cargo of pelts for twelve cents each, which he later sold in China for $120 apiece. British trading vessels swarmed to the Northwest Coast. Their appearance brought Spanish warships to Nootka (1789) and precipitated a controversy that was settled by ceding Nootka to the British.

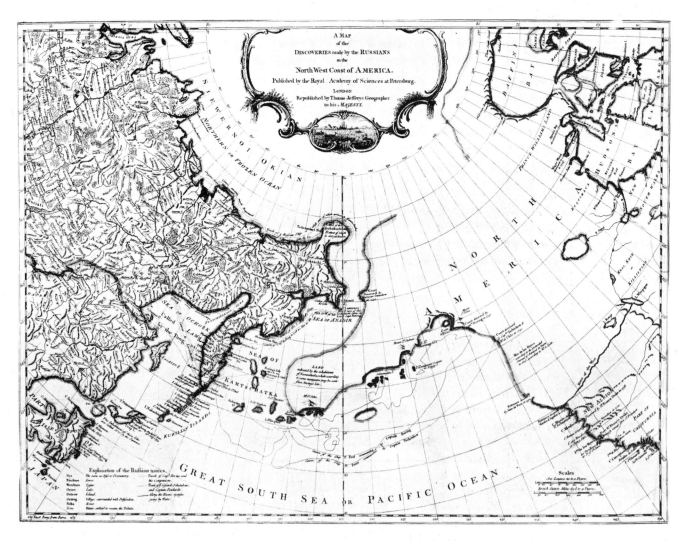

In the 1750's, the Russians knew more about the northern frontiers of New Spain than the Spaniards, as indicated by this map originally published in St. Petersburg in 1758, eleven years before Spain colonized upper California.

Russian settlement in Sitka, Alaska (1799), was one of several bases established by the fur traders. Sitka became headquarters for the Russian American Fur Trading Company, which masterminded operations in California.

Northernmost settlement in Spanish California was Nootka Inlet, on the west coast of Vancouver Island, occupied for five years (1789-94) as a bastion against Russian and English advances. It was lost to England after a showdown. The many Spanish place names in Puget Sound area date from this interlude.

30,000 B.C.–1769

Indian Eden

THE Europeans plotting in distant capitals to occupy California knew pitifully little about the land or its inhabitants. Only three maritime expeditions had come ashore within the span of three centuries, and although they had made contact with the Indians, the meetings had been perfunctory and communications limited to sign language. None of the explorers sent reconnaissance teams inland, and the total knowledge of the land was what could be seen and charted from the deck of a vessel.

Thus, the colonizing parties being assembled in New Spain to invade California were destined to serve as explorers as well as colonists. Although they would not recognize it as such, they were to stumble into a primitive Eden, happily occupied by Indians who had successfully and peacefully lived in it for millenniums.

The Indians had long ago made a practical compact with nature and were effectively living off the fruits of the land. Sheltered by great natural orchards of oaks that showered down an abundance of edible acorns every fall, with a plenitude of game and fish for the taking, and natural gardens of berries and fruiting shrubs, the Indians had little need to plant crops or tend herds to support themselves. True, their search for food was sometimes an hour-by-hour preoccupation, but there was generally enough to go around, and they seldom suf-

Indian women wore skirts of reeds, which swished as they walked, often with an overskirt of deerskin. In cold weather they added a cape of deerskin or rabbit fur. For ornament, they adorned themselves with shells, feathers, and bone.

fered the pangs of starvation. Hungry they might be, but the threat of famine rarely darkened their lives (as it soon did their European conquerors).

The variety and abundance of natural foodstuffs, coupled with a gentle climate, permitted a great concentration of people to live on the land. Experts place the number of Indians living in what is now California at 150,000 to 200,000—more than twice the number per square mile in the Great Plains or along the eastern seaboard.

The first Californians were distributed in a mosaic of comparatively small tribes. Although they shared common cultural patterns in shelter, clothing, hunting techniques, even mythology, they spoke more than twenty-six different languages, some as disparate as modern French from German. Sign language probably bridged the gap to some degree, but the tribes lived a self-contained existence with only minor communication with their neighbors.

Despite language barriers, they were somehow acquainted with the attainments of other native populations as far south as Peru. They knew about the Spaniards long before the white men arrived in their midst; inland tribes had heard of the "floating houses" that had sailed by the coast, and coastal Indians knew about the presence of white men east of the desert. It is possible that this news was disseminated through the channels for exchanging goods.

Tribes swapped goods with those adjoining, and by this method objects were sometimes carried long distances through a succession of ownerships. For instance, much of the obsidian used for arrow tips and spear points in the Central Valley came from a single source near Mono Lake. The heavy chunks

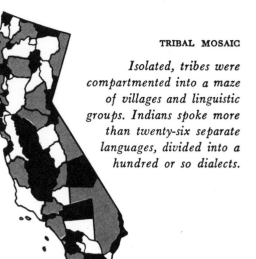

TRIBAL MOSAIC

Isolated, tribes were compartmented into a maze of villages and linguistic groups. Indians spoke more than twenty-six separate languages, divided into a hundred or so dialects.

TRADE ROUTES

Trade between neighboring tribes tended to compensate for tribal isolation. Items of trade passed by successive stages from one tribe to the next. Routes also served as news channels.

were carried over the Sierra passes on the backs of porters and thence dispersed to all the tribes.

Some tribes were highly conscious of material wealth. Within these groups, individuals achieved status by amassing treasure in rare natural objects. The supreme status symbol was a large obsidian blade, possessed only by chiefs or shamans and used in ceremonial rites. Rarest of the rare was red obsidian, a possession equivalent to a crown jewel. Ownership of such a treasure was known far and wide, and no man parted with it without dire provocation. Strings of seashells (dentalia) served as the universal coinage. Strung according to size on cords of standard length, they had as precise a monetary value as the common currencies of today (see chart). Other items of precious worth: the red topknot from woodpecker scalps, albino deerskin, feathered capes, charm stones, and ceremonial baskets.

The tribes lived peaceably with each other, seldom venturing from their pockets of land. If they traveled at all, individuals visited only the tribes immediately surrounding. There was little need to travel to other lands or to covet the possessions of other tribes. Tribal preserves generally supplied sufficient foodstuffs for subsistence, and the possessions of individuals were regarded as inviolate. Two common incitements to military adventure were thus lacking throughout the land.

Not that war was unknown. Nearly all the tribes engaged in occasional battles, and most of the men were schooled in the violent techniques of close-in combat. Skirmishes commonly resulted from a grievance, such as murder, wife stealing, poaching, or thievery. The battles were brief, every-man-for-himself melees that ended as soon as one or two of the warriors were slain or wounded. Honor satisfied, the winner could leave the field with dignity—unless, as often happened, new slights were generated in the heat of conflict, calling for return engagements ad infinitum.

Only the Yumans along the Colorado River practiced organized warfare. Seemingly, they relished fighting for its own sake and would launch forays complete with technical specialists: archers, spearmen, clubmen, a shaman, and a scalp taker. Raiding parties would travel for four or five days to reach a traditional enemy (usually the Mohaves), attack before dawn, kill the warriors, and return with women and children captives.

In many instances, grievances were assuaged bloodlessly by monetary payment, computed according to a highly sophisticated value system. The loss of a chief, for instance, might be compensated by payment of several strings of dentalia, woodpecker scalps, deerskins, obsidian blades, ceremonial baskets, and perhaps a debt slave or two. Even in warfare, the victors sometimes found themselves paying exorbitant tribute to compensate for people killed or maimed or property destroyed.

The Indians lived at peace with their environment as well, fully utilizing their natural resources but without plundering their stocks of game, fish, or timber. They fashioned clothing and shelter from available materials to suit the climate. Men usually went naked, except in cold weather, acting as one later observer noted "as though they were proud of the suit that nature gave them." Women usually wore skirts of deerskin or reeds.

Typical of cultures that do not have to endure great hardship to survive, the Indians were free to channel some of their energies into developments requiring much subtlety and imagination. Elaborate rites revolved around natural phenomena: the annual renewal of the earth in spring, the coming of the acorn crop, and the personal crises of birth, puberty, marriage, and death. Under the guidance of shamans, rites involved fasting or drugs to induce dreams and visions. In the desert areas, psychedelic drugs were widely used under controlled conditions in religious ceremonies.

The shamans also served as the tribal physicians. Following the general belief that illness was caused by some malevolent element in nature, they drew it out of the invalid with incantations. The original homeopathists, they also treated the ill with powders and potions developed from weeds, berries, and roots. The therapeutic value of many of these remedies was well established; in fact, the Spanish doctors found some of them more effective than the remedies they brought with them, and several of them later found their way into the U. S. Pharmacopoeia.

Ritualistic dancing was the usual climax to any religious ceremony. Performed by elaborately costumed men, the dance patterns were repetitive and deceptively simple, but as stylized as figure skating. Accompanied by the beat of a log drum and the fluttering notes from bone whistles, the marathon performance often lasted for several days and nights. One legend tells of a tribe that became "dance mad" and happily danced around the world.

An infectious passion for gambling provided a social outlet for both men and women throughout all the tribes. Willing to bet on any event with the faintest odds on its outcome—such as an athletic contest, a battle, last man out of the sweat house, how many sticks behind the back, or the roll of nutshell dice—whatever the excuse, the Indians took to it with relish. Gambling games were enlivened by singing, dancing, and gamesmanship to discommode the players. Stakes were sometimes high, and dedicated gamblers lost considerable treasure, including an occasional wife.

This then was roughly the shape of the Indian culture that had lasted with little spectacular change for ten thousand years but was soon to be challenged and then virtually destroyed in less than a century. An intelligent and individualistic people, going about their uncomplicated lives, were fated to find themselves strangers in their ancestral lands, their numbers cut in half by the actions of hostile and well-meaning strangers, and their established ways of life fragmented by an alien culture.

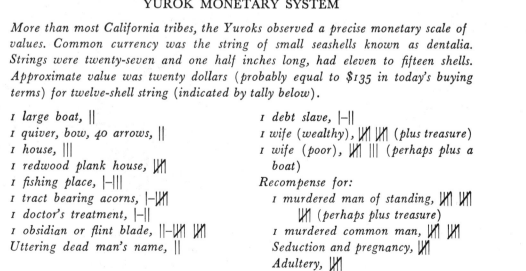

YUROK MONETARY SYSTEM

More than most California tribes, the Yuroks observed a precise monetary scale of values. Common currency was the string of small seashells known as dentalia. Strings were twenty-seven and one half inches long, had eleven to fifteen shells. Approximate value was twenty dollars (probably equal to $135 in today's buying terms) for twelve-shell string (indicated by tally below).

1 large boat, ||
1 quiver, bow, 40 arrows, ||
1 house, |||
1 redwood plank house, |||||
1 fishing place, |–|||
1 tract bearing acorns, |–|||||
1 doctor's treatment, |–||
1 obsidian or flint blade, ||–||||| |||||
Uttering dead man's name, ||

1 debt slave, |–||
1 wife (wealthy), ||||| ||||| *(plus treasure)*
1 wife (poor), ||||| ||| *(perhaps plus a boat)*
Recompense for:
  1 murdered man of standing, ||||| ||||| ||||| *(perhaps plus treasure)*
  1 murdered common man, ||||| |||||
Seduction and pregnancy, |||||
Adultery, |||||

Shelter to Match the Climate

Living in a land of many climates, the Indians built a variety of house types, each suited to the local climate and the available building materials.

In the damp north woods, they erected warm and reasonably weathertight structures of slabs and boards. In the southern valleys and along the coast, they plaited shelters of reeds over willow frames. In areas of intense summer heat, they dug into the earth and formed shelters of mounded soil to escape the searching sun.

Whether built of wood, reeds, or mud, the houses were universally heated by an open fire in the middle of the floor, vented through a hole in the roof. In the Sacramento Valley, the incombustible natives entered and exited through the smoke hole itself.

Igloo-shaped houses of reeds provided breezy shelter in summer in the temperate areas and were covered with deerskins during the rainy season. Easily whipped together in a few hours, the houses were expendable. When they became infested with vermin, they were burned to the ground and new ones built nearby.

In the northern woodlands, houses large enough for a big family including all the next of kin, were built of boards lashed to a post-and-beam framework. Remarkable feats for Stone Age craftsmen, the structures were assembled without benefit of steel cutting tools.

Slab huts, favored in wooded or mountainous areas, were often formed by leaning splits of redwood, cedar, or pine together with sufficient overlap to shed most of the rain. These were usually built over a pit dug two or three feet into the earth for added warmth.

INDIAN EDEN

Dining Off the Landscape

Surrounded by an abundance and variety of natural foods, the Indians ate reasonably well, and they could readily switch to alternate sources if a staple such as the acorn crop failed to ripen. Along the coast, they consumed shellfish, shore birds, and small game, or feasted on the carcasses of whales washed—or sometimes driven—ashore. Inland, they lived on game, birds, berries, seeds, and acorns. In the desert, cactus fruits, dates, mesquite beans, bulbs, and roots supported a population of thousands.

Part of their diverse diet consisted of foods that would gag Europeans— reptiles, insects, skunks—but the Indians likewise had their taboos. Most tribes would not eat grizzly bear meat (although the cubs were sometimes captured and fattened for eating), they avoided the coyote for religious reasons, eschewed the buzzard for its evil flavor, and avoided mussels during the months of their toxicity.

Adept fishermen, the Indians relied on a variety of gear: hook and line, basket traps, nets, vegetable poisons. Hooks were fashioned from shells, lines from braided plant fibers. Along the ocean shore they developed a proficiency for catching fish with their bare hands—a quicksilvery feat that astonished Drake's chroniclers. So many tons of shellfish were consumed over the centuries that mounds of discarded shells in some village sites are twenty feet thick.

Processing acorns was a domestic specialty of the women, who gathered the nuts in fall, stored them in granaries (above), and pounded them into meal (right) in stone mortars or in communal grinding rocks. They then leached the meal in hot water to remove the tannic acid. The flour was served in many ways: the dried raw cake was eaten in that state; broken up and mixed with water, it made a soup; and, cooked in boiling water, it became porridge. The meal was rarely flavored or seasoned. An estimated two thousand pounds of acorns were needed per Indian per year.

ACORN MEAL: BREAKFAST OF BRAVES

Acorns have been a staple food since ancient times in all parts of the world. Wars have been fought for possession of acorn groves. Popular in Spain —even today—the nuts were a fashionable fillip for high society in Madrid in the 1800's. Highly nutritional, the acorn provides "starch, fixed oil, citric acid, and sugar, as well as astringent and bitter principles." The largest and most palatable acorn in California came from the white oak (Quercus lobata), but the Indians' practice of leaching after pulverizing made even the bitterest kinds edible; the women harvested fourteen varieties.

Nutritional Comparison with Modern Cereals

	Acorn Meal	Cream of Wheat	Quaker Oats
Fat	21.3%	1.2%	6.0%
Protein	5.1	11.9	15.0
Carbohydrates	62.2	73.0	66.0

Master Craftsmanship

Two extraordinary accomplishments in handcrafts place the California Indians high in the rankings of American tribes. Proficient in many hand arts, they excelled in basketry and canoemaking.

Baskets were a practical necessity for cooking, storing, and carrying. Woven with great care and elegantly ornamented, they were made to serve specialized functions. Basket-weaving techniques were also used in fashioning game traps and fishing weirs.

Of the various types of watercraft used by the coastal and river tribes, a seagoing canoe made by the Chumash near Santa Barbara is rated as one of the finest vessels in the New World. Formed of planks, these boats could range freely over open sea sixty miles to the offshore islands. Light and maneuverable, the vessels impressed Vizcaíno, who noted that "they seemed to fly."

Baskets, formed either by twining, as above, or by coiling, were made by the women of every tribe. Most proficient were the Pomo women, who produced baskets of such elegance that they were prized throughout all the tribes and were traded far and wide. Designs woven into the fiber were invariably geometric, not symbolic. Ornamentation of feathers and opalescent bits of shell were often added.

Sampling of specialized baskets: (A) baby carriers, (B) storage containers, and (C) treasure baskets. Other types included: asphalt-lined water bottles (up to five gallons), winnowing trays, hats, gambling trays, parching trays, and cooking vessels. Food was boiled in watertight baskets by dropping heated stones into the mixture and stirring madly to keep them from burning the fiber.

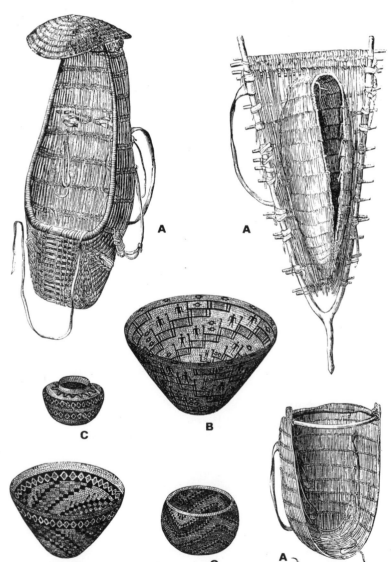

Three main types of watercraft: Reed rafts (above) were expendable craft that could be quickly bundled together. They remained buoyant only as long as the reeds stayed dry; once they became waterlogged, the rafts foundered. General rule was not to tarry when rowing one of these. Dugouts (right) were fashioned from downed trees or driftwood logs. With infinite patience, the Indians burned and scraped out a hollow with sharpened elkhorn, clamshells, or obsidian blades. Clumsy but durable, they lasted for years. Plank canoes (right) of the Chumash were both fine pieces of craftsmanship and very seaworthy vessels. The planks were smoothed with stone or clamshell scrapers, calked with pitch, and sewn together with fiber cord laced through holes drilled in the wood. Ranging from fourteen to twenty-four feet in length, they usually carried only two rowers and a boy for bailing, but they could transport fifteen or twenty on long voyages over open water.

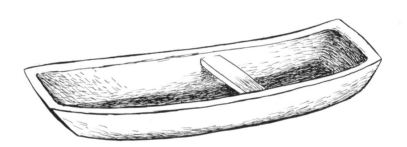

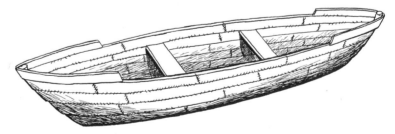

Dancers decorated with tattoos, stripes of red, black, and white body paint, one covered with feathers held in place with tar, perform at San Jose. Bright apparel was worn by dancers of either sex.

Lively Tribal Heritage

Tribal wisdom and philosophy were embodied in a rich heritage of myths and legends handed down orally and expressed visually in ritual dances and sand paintings.

Essential to a meaningful life, the myths explained in naturalistic terms the origins of the world and its people, the causes of earthquake, fire, and flood, the cycles of renewal and death, and the actions of important deities. Legends carried forward the history of the tribe, perpetuating the great events of the past, real or imagined.

Of indirect religious significance but still a rooted part of tribal life was the men-only institution of the sweat house, a kind of community sauna, where men gathered to dream, talk, and loaf.

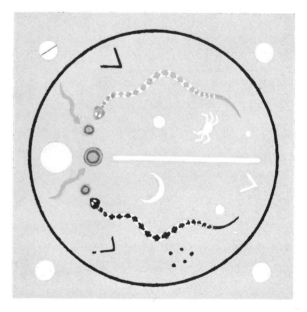

The sweathouse (temescal) was a dominant feature
of every village, a kind of therapeutic men's club.
Within it a fire was kept burning at all times, and
men would gather around it to perspire in the dry
heat (right). When they were sweating profusely,
they would dash outside and fling themselves into a
nearby lake or stream (above). It served as a
purification rite before or after battle or a ritual
dance, as a cleansing agent to remove man scent
from hunters about to stalk game, as a health
measure, as a place to conjure visions, or simply, a
haven where the men could sequester themselves
away from the women and children. Usually of
considerable hygienic benefit, the temescal became
a death trap in mission days when stricken Indians
gathered there to recover from measles and smallpox.

Sand paintings, used in psychedelic rites by desert tribes, depicted the meaning of
life. Diegueño painting (left) shows the visible world, peopled with friendly and
hostile creatures, under summer and winter constellations. Most popular constellation
was the Pleiades, known to many tribes as The Maidens.

Spanish Transplant

On a spring day in 1769, a small vessel sailed uncertainly into the bay of San Diego, dropped anchor, and the crew awkwardly furled its sails.

To the excited Indians watching its arrival, the "house with wings" was a frightening apparition, for most of them had never seen a sailing ship before.

To the skeletons on board, the landfall marked release from a disastrous fifty-five-day voyage. All but two of the crew and passengers were sick or disabled, victims of scurvy. The ailing men scarcely looked like the advance guard of a powerful and haughty nation, sent to subdue and settle this land. But the stricken seamen, half dead with disease, were the forerunners of an invasion that would transform the lives of the Indians and ultimately lead to their near extinction.

The leaky frigate *San Antonio* carried one contingent of a four-party Spanish expedition sent to colonize Upper California. Plans for the great expedition had been proposed to King Charles III in minute detail the year before and enthusiastically approved.

The colonizing venture fitted into the king's grand strategy to forestall Russian occupation of Spain's long-neglected territory in California. The monarch had ascended the throne in the dying days

A piece of Europe stranded on a distant shore, the Franciscan mission stands as a monument to the zealous Spaniards who played out the closing drama of their once-mighty empire in this lonely outpost. Mission San Buenaventura was a thriving medieval city, autocratic and anachronistic.

of the great empire and had instilled a vigor not seen for decades—nor seen again after his reign.

Among his most significant improvements was the appointment of capable men to replace the deadheads lodged in positions of authority, and one of the best of his choices was the *visitador general,* José de Gálvez, whom he dispatched to New Spain in 1765. Gálvez served for only six years, but during this brief stay he introduced a number of sweeping changes in the administration of the frontier and, most important, organized and launched the astonishingly successful California expedition.

Plans for the settlement were taken from stock. Over the centuries, Spain had developed standard methods for settling new territory, based on a close co-operation between religious and military authorities. In lands where native hostility was anticipated, the sword cleared the way, and once the natives had been conquered, missionaries brought the benefits of Christianity to the survivors. This was the approach in Mexico. In other areas, where the natives were known to be peace-loving, the missionaries led the way, accompanied by a small body of soldiers for protection and police assistance. This was the approach selected for California.

Conquest by teams of priests and soldiers was an economical and proven means of subduing a new country. The operation took only a handful of dedicated and forceful men who could live off the land or subsist on a trickle of supplies brought by mule train or sailing vessel. With blandishments of bright beads, cloth, and food, the missionaries wooed the natives to Christianity, and once they had persuaded them to accept the commitment, they drove

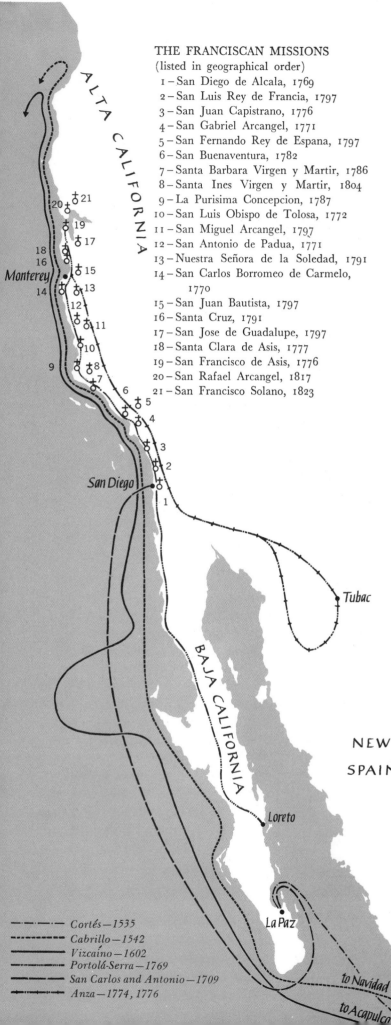

THE FRANCISCAN MISSIONS
(listed in geographical order)

1 – San Diego de Alcala, 1769
2 – San Luis Rey de Francia, 1797
3 – San Juan Capistrano, 1776
4 – San Gabriel Arcangel, 1771
5 – San Fernando Rey de Espana, 1797
6 – San Buenaventura, 1782
7 – Santa Barbara Virgen y Martir, 1786
8 – Santa Ines Virgen y Martir, 1804
9 – La Purisima Concepcion, 1787
10 – San Luis Obispo de Tolosa, 1772
11 – San Miguel Arcangel, 1797
12 – San Antonio de Padua, 1771
13 – Nuestra Señora de la Soledad, 1791
14 – San Carlos Borromeo de Carmelo, 1770
15 – San Juan Bautista, 1797
16 – Santa Cruz, 1791
17 – San Jose de Guadalupe, 1797
18 – Santa Clara de Asis, 1777
19 – San Francisco de Asis, 1776
20 – San Rafael Arcangel, 1817
21 – San Francisco Solano, 1823

Cortés – 1535
Cabrillo – 1542
Vizcaíno – 1602
Portolá-Serra – 1769
San Carlos and Antonio – 1709
Anza – 1774, 1776

them mercilessly to produce for God and the Crown.

They taught the Indians rudimentary handcrafts, introduced them to agriculture and the raising of cattle, and prepared them for the day when they would eventually take over the missions as free men.

Following—or alongside—the mission compounds were the pueblos, the second stage in the grand colonial plan. Pueblos were packaged towns, planned in advance with painstaking care by the Spaniards, who recruited inhabitants in New Spain (mission Indians were excluded) and sent them north on the long trail. Pueblos were planned as agricultural centers, cow towns, occupied by experienced farmers and herdsmen, who raised their crops and grazed their herds in the domains outside of the town.

The actual colonization of California was initiated by a two-pronged expedition dispatched from La Paz. Land parties herded cattle and horses with them; ships carried food, equipment, hardware, and church supplies too bulky to carry on muleback.

The combined expedition was commanded by the Governor of Baja California, Don Gaspar de Portolá, relieved of his duties to direct this important assignment. Under him, responsible for spiritual matters, was Father Junípero Serra, a zealous Spaniard with thirty-five years' experience in the frontiers of New Spain.

The expedition was charged with the immediate objective of finding the great harbor of Monterey, glowingly described by Vizcaíno 167 years earlier, and there establishing the first of a series of mission settlements. The four parties met in San Diego, decimated by sickness and death, and a weary detachment continued northward and eventually lo-

The twenty-one missions were founded in three waves. First, anchor missions were located near the coast for easy supply by ship. The next group was founded in between, a day's march apart. The third group was located farther inland. Another chain, planned for the Central Valley, was blocked by Mexican revolt. Supplies from New Spain were carried over tenuous and treacherous routes: the land trail up the peninsula was abandoned as too arid to support mule trains. The sea route, backbone of supply, was plagued by bad weather and scurvy that killed crews.

Monarch of California, King Charles III of Spain, goaded the faltering empire into a semblance of its former glory. He authorized colonization of California to block Russia from seizing the land and England from dominating the Pacific rim. A candid portrait by Goya reveals the king as a lonely old man, a clownlike figure in hunting togs.

cated Monterey. As an incidental by-product of the first expedition, the party stumbled on the far more important bay of San Francisco, sighting it for the first time in recorded history.

At the start, the dual authority shared by Serra and Portolá functioned smoothly because the two men worked well together. But the double yoke later proved irksome. The royal instruction called for a single authority in the governor, who was responsible only to the Crown; but within the socioeconomic frame of the missions, the line between spiritual and temporal authority was often paper thin.

The Spaniards found the Indians resistant to conversion. No matter that the natives were accustomed to a far different way of life; all within the path of the newcomers were swept into the mission system, and the Indians' tribal cultures were pushed aside. A few of the friars took special interest in their charges' primitive life patterns. Some learned the native tongues so they could teach them the Mass. Some applied the tools of sociological scholarship to their languages and customs and left an important record of the mission tribes.

White man's diseases stalked the Indians. Thousands died of measles and chicken pox, and hundreds more fell prey to venereal disease introduced by the soldiers and sailors.

Nevertheless, despite seemingly insurmountable obstacles, the padres were able to persuade thousands of Indians to accept the benevolent despotism of the mission system, and under their prodding, often backed by the threat of punishment, the Indians developed the missions into amazingly successful operations. So successful, in fact, that they sealed their own doom. As the economic mainstay of the province, their crops, handcrafts, foodstuffs, and livestock aroused the cupidity of a growing

population of colonists outside the mission compounds. When the ties of authority were loosened by revolution in Mexico, the church was unable to protect the missions from despoliation, and after sixty-five years of operation they were disbanded beginning in 1834.

Detractors of the mission system condemn it on the grounds that it was outright slavery cloaked in pious disguise, that it destroyed an existing native culture without replacing it with a better way of life, and that it brought the Indians into the modern mainstream without adequate preparation.

All these charges are easily documented. However, in fairness to the dedicated men who built and ran the missions, it can be pointed out that slavery was an accepted colonial institution of the eighteenth century—indeed, it persisted in the United States for three decades after the missions were secularized—and that the padres' main concern was a genuine desire to elevate the Indians to a place in modern society.

A bantamweight friar from Majorca, the venerated Father Junípero Serra headed the spiritual side of the California expedition.

For God and King

Failure and disaster haunted the founding of Spanish California. The first colonists to arrive were cut down by death and disease, and the survivors were barely capable of building shelter to protect themselves from the Indians and the elements. Facing starvation when the supply ships were delayed, they almost turned back.

Nevertheless, Father Serra dedicated the first mission at San Diego in 1769 and Portolá fulfilled his orders to find Monterey Bay a few weeks later. It took Portolá two tries to find the mythical bay because it had been oversold by its imaginative discoverer, Vizcaíno, 167 years before. Convinced that the windswept crescent was indeed the "fair great harbour," Portolá and Serra dedicated the headquarters mission there in 1770, and Portolá sailed for Mexico City and out of the pages of history. Serra remained, serving tirelessly until his death at Carmel Mission fourteen years later.

A noble Castilian, Don Gaspar de Portolá, held the over-all authority at the start. The assignment was a welcome relief from an empty governorship in Baja California.

The ceremony of founding a mission followed the centuries-old ritual. The ranking civil authority took possession of the land for the Crown, raising a handful of soil and planting the flagstaff in the dirt. The ranking ecclesiastic claimed the subjects for God, sang the Mass, and delivered a sermon. Not all of the founding ceremonies were as elaborate as the start of Mission San Carlos Borromeo, at Monterey, as pictured above. The founding of this mission had been the shining goal of the entire expedition, and in recognition of the importance of the occasion, troops and sailors were assembled in formation around the altar and cannon on shipboard punctuated the Mass with rolling volleys that sent the curious Indians fleeing to the cypress woods. When news of this great day reached Mexico City, every church bell in the capital pealed out the good tidings.

Dancing before new gods, Indians perform a pagan rite within the shadow of Mission Dolores to celebrate a saint's day in 1816. Most of the padres tolerated a mild residue of paganism in their converts, channeled some of it into church festivals, and looked the other way when distraught Indians invoked their old gods in times of deep trouble.

Clash of Cultures

On top of an Indian culture unchanged since the Stone Age, the Spaniards imposed the autocratic ways of eighteenth-century Spain. In a scant sixty years, they induced thousands of Indians to leave behind their stone tools and weapons, their nakedness, their tribal identities, and their abundant natural foodstuffs.

From independent, free-circulating hunters and fishermen, the mission Indians became virtual slaves, confined within the compounds and impressed into labor details. From nature worshipers they were converted into nominal Christians, capable of celebrating the Mass but without comprehension.

The change was too drastic for many. Some shirked, some rebelled, some fled to the hills. The missionaries complained that the Indians were unusually resistant to learning new ways, and the padres postponed the day when the missions would be turned over to the converts to operate.

Ten millenniums of feeling and technique stand between the Indian rock paintings and the scene of Christ's agonizing ascent of Calvary (above), one of twelve oil paintings by a mission convert rendered in the early 1800's and still on display at San Gabriel. Under the tutelage of the padres and imported artists, adept Indians crossed a cultural abyss and learned to portray the complex symbols and scenes of Christianity in the manner of eighteenth-century Europeans for the embellishment of altars, pulpits, and chapel walls.

Commemorative basket woven by an Indian woman for dedication of Mission San Buenaventura (1782) incorporates Spanish royal coat of arms in its design. Basket was sent to Mexico City, where it remained for a century.

Unforeseen and irreversible, the gift of death came with the white men, who brought diseases for which the Indians had no immunity. Measles killed thousands; hundreds more died of smallpox and syphilis. The plaque in the cemetery at Mission Dolores memorializes 5512 Indians who died there.

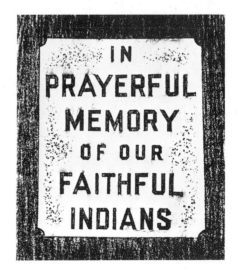

IN PRAYERFUL MEMORY OF OUR FAITHFUL INDIANS

Forced Compliance

Not every native Californian welcomed the Spaniards to his land. Hundreds never accepted the mission yoke and some that did rebelled against the strict discipline.

The thoroughgoing Spaniards had anticipated such perfidy and sent soldiers along with the padres to protect the missions from Indian attack and to punish converts who broke the stringent rules.

In actuality, the soldiers caused more trouble than they settled. A brutish lot, sprung from Mexican jails, they mistreated the Indians, molested the women, and introduced crippling diseases. Had the peaceful Indians been versed in military organization and tactics, they could easily have expelled the invaders, whom they outnumbered a hundred to one, but, lacking such discipline, they were held in uneasy check by a token force of some four hundred "leather jackets" scattered over the province.

On a dark night in 1784 the first major Indian revolt in Spanish California flared into violence at San Diego. An undisciplined mob of four hundred braves swept down upon the mission, set fire to the buildings, killed two colonists, and martyred a missionary, Father Jaime. The settlers fled to the presidio six miles down the canyon, and did not return to the original site for ten years. But the fact that an attack of such magnitude had failed intimidated the Indians, and they never again attempted a large raid.

Spanish dragoon shown in battle with Indian
bowmen in a 1791 drawing had the advantages of
arrow-proof leather armor and the company of a
horse, a fearsome apparition to the Indians who had
never seen such an animal. Once they had overcome
their awe of the mounted soldiers, however, the
Indians outside the mission territory harassed them
effectively with their simple weapons and repelled
several punitive forays sent against them.

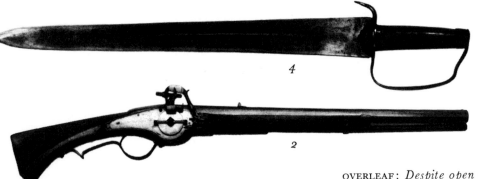

3

1

4

2

Tools of the military trade:
*1. bullhide shield to ward off
arrows; 2. musket—no
match for bow and arrow;
3. powder charges;
4. cavalry saber.*

OVERLEAF: *Despite open and covert opposition of the Indians,
the missions in their heyday were centers of intense activity.
For relief from the daily grind, the padres encouraged
celebrations such as the chastising of Judas during Easter
Week at Mission Dolores.*

Indians who had never used steel tools before were taught a dozen crafts in the process of building the big rambling missions. Progress was slow, but the padres had plenty of time. Some of the mission complexes took ten to fifteen years of patient toil for completion.

Up from the Soil

Thrown on their own resources, the padres ordered the building of the missions literally from the ground up.

The first structures were stockades, walled with stakes and roofed with thatch. Drafty and leaky, they were replaced with buildings formed of blocks of sun-dried mud (adobes) made by the hundreds of thousands. The blocks were made by puddling soil into a thick soup, adding manure and straw as a binder, and pouring into a wooden mold. Virtually living walls, the adobes were known to sprout wild flowers after spring rains. Some bricks sent to the Harvard Medical School in the 1930's were found to be harboring smallpox germs, still viable after 139 years.

More durable masonry needed for flues, fireplaces, roofing, patio flooring, and water pipes was kiln-fired. Pipe lengths were thrown on a potter's wheel, and roof tiles were shaped over wooden molds—not over the thighs of Indians, as legend persists (the twenty-four-inch tiles would have required the services of Indians ten feet tall!).

Following 1790, contingents of master masons from Mexico arrived in the province and directed the building of magnificent stone churches at Carmel, Santa Barbara, San Gabriel, and San Juan Capistrano.

When the Malaspina scientific expedition from Spain visited Carmel Mission in 1791, the compound was beginning to take its final form, but work had not yet started on the beautiful stone church. Buildings were still roofed with thatch, a material that was soon replaced by tile throughout the mission chain. First tile roof was installed at San Luis Obispo in 1791 as protection against fire raids.

Mission compounds were miniature medieval walled cities, complete with all the necessary crafts and living quarters for self-support. Built in a quadrangle around an open square, the structures usually contained a chapel, shops, living quarters for padres and guests, an infirmary, single-women's lodging, cooking and dining facilities. As this plan of Mission San Luis Rey indicates, the chapel, which is all that remains at most missions, was just one part of the large complex.

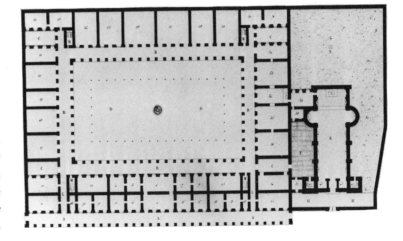

Most extensive of the four presidios, the one at Monterey was built in 1771, remodeled in 1810, and not completed until 1834. Within its walls were quarters for troops and officers, a jail, and the royal chapel, which is still in use. A powder magazine was located a league to the south.

Frontier Forts

With freebooters roaming the seas, attacking Spanish ships and ports, and Russian colonists moving down from Alaska, military protection for Alta California was mandatory. Presidios (forts) were immediately established at the ports of San Diego and Monterey to guard both ends of the colony. Discovery of San Francisco Bay prompted the addition of a third bastion, and a fourth was built in Santa Barbara, midpoint of the mission chain.

The first presidios were crude log stockades, adequate protection from Indian arrows but not against ship-borne cannon. Redoubts of stone and adobe later replaced the wooden shelters. Each presidio had a shore battery on an eminence where it could sweep the harbor of hostile ships.

Starved for funds and staffed largely with riffraff, the presidios were militarily impotent, but they did offer a potential threat to foreign adventurers.

Pirate-patriot Hippolyte Bouchard exchanged volleys with artillerymen in Monterey and Santa Barbara when he visited the ports in 1818 in an attempt to persuade Californians to declare their independence of Spain. Unready for such a treasonous move (which in fact came two years later), the Californians rebuffed him, carried on a desultory artillery duel, and suffered the sacking of Monterey in retaliation. Bouchard's naked Kanaka sailors returned to the ship dressed in Spanish garb.

The shore battery guarding the Golden Gate from its lofty perch three miles west of the San Francisco presidio was originally armed with only two eight-pounders. A sixfold increase in armament was effected after the commandant visited the Russian fort at Bodega and saw the formidable caliber of its guns.

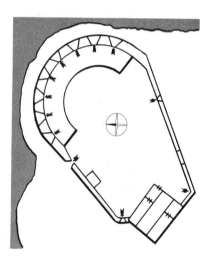

The ground plan for the San Francisco battery called for training the cannon on the Golden Gate. Properly manned, the guns would have kept any hostile craft from entering the bay, but the ordnance was allowed to deteriorate for lack of funds. During the war with Mexico, Frémont spiked the guns under cover of darkness. The raiding party did its job so well that the touchholes of some of the cannon are plugged to this day.

The dress uniform of the Catalan infantryman, assigned to the presidios to strengthen the garrisons, was a handsome outfit—while it lasted. So poorly were the troops paid and provisioned that their uniforms were never replaced after they wore out. So short was the military budget that gunpowder had to be borrowed from private sources before punitive forays could take to the field. A welcoming salute for a foreign ship once had to be deferred until a charge could be borrowed from the vessel itself!

Towns to Order

Soon after the founding of the first missions and presidios, the viceroy ordered the establishment of pueblos and farming communities to bolster the struggling colony. Since colonial policy required that such settlements be populated by established families, a way had to be found to safely move a large number of people with their livestock and supplies from New Spain to Alta California. The few supply ships shuttling back and forth could barely keep the missions and presidios stocked, let alone transport hundreds of farmers and their cattle. A practical land route was needed, and a venturesome lieutenant in the border command, Juan Bautista de Anza, was ordered to find one. In a brilliant performance, the young officer led two large parties across trackless desert and mountains and delivered them safely in Monterey and in Yerba Buena, as San Francisco was named at the time. Anza's route was closed soon afterward when Indians massacred a third party of colonists at the Colorado River.

"A man of heroic qualities, tough as oak, and silent as the desert from which he sprang," Juan Bautista de Anza blazed an overland trail from Sonora, Mexico, to Monterey in 1774 and two years later successfully shepherded 240 colonists, 500 horses, and 300 head of cattle 700 miles over the same route in the dead of winter, arriving in Monterey with two more souls than the initial roster. In honor of his achievements, Anza's name has been bestowed upon a town, a desert, streets, parks, schools, and a junior college.

Typical of Spanish thoroughness, advance estimates of the equipment needs and costs were prepared for the Anza marches. The "minute calculation" for the second expedition listed a hundred items, valued at 22,000 pesos, needed to sustain a party of 240 men, women, and children (180 of the last-mentioned) for the forty-day trip. Sample entries:

EQUIPAGE FOR THE LONG TRAIL

Wardrobe for a Woman
3 shirts
3 pairs of white Puebla petticoats
2 pairs of petticoats, some of silk serge, others of thick flannel, and an underskirt
2 varas of linen stuff for two linings
2 pairs of Brussels stockings
2 pairs of hose
2 pairs of shoes
2 women's shawls

1 hat
6 varas of ribbon

Gifts for Indians included the following pacifiers: 6 cases of glass beads that contain no black and abound in red, 600 war clubs, 350 pounds of highest grade tobacco.

Cattle and Provisions to Ration the People of the Expedition
100 head of cattle, one for each day

30 loads of flour for tortillas
60 fanegas of pinole
60 fanegas of kidney beans
6 cases of ordinary chocolate
2 tercios of white sugar
12 pesos' worth of soap
3 barrels of *aguardiente* for necessities

Table for the Commandant and Chaplain
added to the above: pork sausage, biscuits, fine chocolate, wine, cheese, seasonings.

The last settlement to be founded, Sonoma was established by Mariano Vallejo in
1835 under the Mexican regime. Troops shown drilling in the plaza were from the
San Francisco presidio, transferred to strengthen the defenses against the Russian
colony thirty miles to the north. The plaza, depicted here with considerable artistic
license, was the setting for the Bear Flag revolt eleven years later.

The second pueblo to be founded in the
province, Los Angeles was settled in 1781
by eleven reluctant families who had been
enticed from Sonora by the promise of an
abundant life in California. Half jailbirds,
half farmers, the motley group worked
together to develop a highly successful
agricultural community which nearly
outproduced the nearby Mission San
Gabriel with its hundreds of Indians.

Death of the Missions

Secular use of mission buildings was commonplace. Purisima, above, served as headquarters for a sheep ranch; other mission buildings were desecrated as hotels, restaurants, bars, residences, barracks, stores, warehouses, and a house of ill fame.

Begun in 1834, secularization of the missions had far-reaching effects—partly beneficial, mostly disastrous. The change marked a transfer of authority to lay officials from the Franciscans, who refused allegiance to the revolutionary regime in Mexico and returned home. It marked the breakup of eight million acres of mission land into eight hundred privately owned ranchos. The economy built on mission production was destroyed—orchards chopped down for firewood, herds dispersed into private hands, and crops lost for lack of care. Further, the influence of Hispanic Catholicism in California sank to a low ebb from which it did not recover for half a century.

Hardest hit by the cataclysm were the mission Indians, who, suddenly released from authoritarian security, found themselves ill-prepared to cope with freedom. They returned to the hills, indentured themselves as ranch hands, or turned to drink or gambling.

Services were held in some of the crumbling churches for years after secularization. A priest visited Carmel, above, once a month to bring the Mass to loyal converts. In a few of the mission churches, notably Santa Barbara, services have continued regularly and without a break to the present day.

Somber portrayal of an abandoned mission, sketched in 1850, captures the woeful appearance of the missions that were deactivated for lack of parishioners and priests to serve them. Roof tiles, hardware, and fittings were sold or stolen and the unprotected walls left to dissolve in the rain. Agitation for restoring the decaying churches, initiated by concerned Protestants, began in the 1870's and has been proceeding ever since. All of the chapels are now restored, with widely varying degrees of authenticity.

A workaday task of the California vaquero was roping potential saddle stock from racing herds of wild horses, descendants of the first remudas brought from Mexico in the 1770's. With a plentiful supply of horses near at hand, vaqueros felt no need to take care of their ponies, rode them hard until they faltered, then discarded them for fresh mounts. Herds of outlaw horses proliferated, and mustangs were destroyed by the hundreds in annual roundups because they grazed off forage needed for the more valuable cattle.

1830–1850

Restless Pastorale

For two turbulent decades following Mexico's break from Spain in 1821, California was left alone to improvise its own destiny. The harassed central government in Mexico City was too beset by revolutionary turmoil to do more than send a sequence of governors and some ragtag soldiers north.

Left to itself, the province went through years of ferment that dimly reflected the travail then wracking Spain's collapsing empire but without the mindless bloodletting that darkened the liberaion movements to the south. The years in California saw the transfer of authority from medieval monarchy to modern republic, from a church-dominated mission system to a privately owned rancho economy, and, most important, from authoritarian central government to a prideful self-determinaion.

The effects of Mexico's severance from Spain were slow to penetrate to far-off California. Six months after Mexico's formal break, the news reached Monterey and all citizens were required to swear allegiance to the new government. The switch in loyalties meant little to most Californians, and they celebrated the change-over with fireworks and fiestas. But not so the Franciscan missionaries. Royalists to a man, the padres remained unflinchingly loyal to the Spanish Crown, even after it had become obvious that Spain would never regain her lost colonies. They refused to recognize the democratic regimes, subverted them when they could, and were ultimately forced to turn over the mission assets to private hands and return home.

The breakup of the missions, from 1832 to 1845, had far-reaching effects. Secularization dissolved a stabilizing force that had kept the colony intact for half a century and had been its economic mainstay. The Mexican governors lost little time in distributing the missions' livestock, croplands, stored food reserves, and pasturage to army veterans, relatives, and friends. Although under the law the land was supposed to revert to the Indians, few of them received any because of mismanagement by the secularizing authorities.

For the Californians who benefited from this largesse, the change was an exhilarating and, to them, overdue improvement in their lot. The social and economic center shifted to the rancho, and the tempo of life changed to that of the frontier cattle range. Raising cattle was a simple and basic way of life that demanded little of its patrons. With no line fences to patrol and repair on the open range, no need for tight surveillance over the branded stock, the vaquero had little to absorb his days, other than to practice feats of horsemanship the better to impress the señoritas. When action was needed, it was expert and violent: rodeos, brandings, slaughterings, wild-horse roundups, and bear hunts relieved the tedium.

Each rancho was a patriarchal enterprise, headquartered in an adobe hacienda where several generations lived in harmony. At the start of the rancho era, most of the adobes were cold, drafty, and cheerless hovels, having no glass windows, doors, or fireplaces and lacking all but the most rudimentary furniture improvised from hides and scraps of lumber. As prosperity increased, civilized amenities were bartered from trading vessels.

Some of the wealthier rancheros, who had made fortunes in the hide and tallow trade, lived in large adobe quadrangles that resembled the mission compounds on a smaller scale. The houses, built around a patio, had living quarters for the family and servants and numerous rooms where Indians made useful goods. Over the years, some of these great houses mellowed into symbols of a romantic way of life, and their form was copied a century later by Westerners seeking a gracious architectural style for large dwellings.

Social life on the ranchos was a continual round of festivals and fandangos, weddings and wakes, races and cockfights. The first Yankee visitors and settlers disapproved of such frivolity, little understanding the Latin temperament. Later arrivals showed a more appreciative attitude toward these carefree years and bestowed evocative names on the era—Days of the Dons, Splendid Idle Forties, Spanish Arcadia, Halcyon Days. These were the years when the "Mexican men and women of degree" lived the "half barbaric, half elegant, wholly generous and free-handed life" described by Helen Hunt Jackson in 1870 in her romantic novel *Ramona*. "The Californians," added appreciative historian H. H. Bancroft, "were kind-hearted and liberal; a person could travel from San Diego to Sonoma without a coin in his pocket, and never want for a roof to cover him, a bed to sleep on, food to eat, and even tobacco to smoke."

While the *gente de razón*—gentlemen of reason, as they called themselves—were consolidating their Arcadia, winds of change were blowing over the province. Soon after the Mexican take-over of New Spain in 1821, the province of Alta California was forced to subsist on its own resources with little help from the central government. The annual supply ships ceased to sail north, funds for paying soldiers, petty officials, and the padres were cut off, and the Californios—a proud name they adopted —found themselves bankrupt and short of supplies. They were forced to consume the production of the disintegrating missions and to barter hides, tallow, and grain with trading vessels for bare necessities. Fortunately, restrictions against foreign trade were lifted and the padres and rancheros could barter freely with the canny ships' captains.

The Mexican government dispatched a series of governors—twelve men served in twenty-four years —some good, some bad, some forced to return home after a few hectic months in office. Further, the government enraged the provincials by shipping convicts and political prisoners to California to dispose of them. The convicts celebrated their new freedom with crime sprees; the political activists fomented revolutions. Fed up, the Californios forced at least one boatload of undesirables to turn around soon after anchoring in San Diego Bay.

Neglected and ignored from the start by Mexico City, provincial politicians began to contend for local power. Seeds of freedom had been planted a few years before, in 1818, when patriot-pirate Hippolyte Bouchard made his unsuccessful attempt to enlist Alta California in the widespreading rebellion against Spain. Within the province, a few young men chanced upon the heretical doctrines of freedom, equality, and fraternity that were tearing

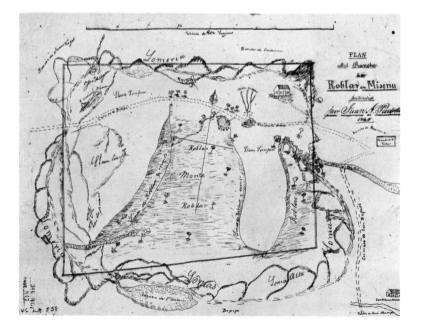

A rough topographical map, or diseño, of a rancho was filed with application for land grant. Loosely defined boundaries were related to landmarks such as trees, streams, houses, and outcroppings, or even coyote burrows, cactus clumps, steers' skulls, and other ephemera. Inexact and inaccurate, the descriptions later made ownership hard to prove in American courts.

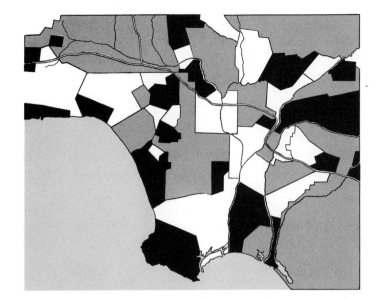

A patchwork of land grants covered nearly all of the Los Angeles basin and some of the foothills. Largest grants are today occupied by entire cities. No more than thirty grants were awarded in California by the Spaniards after 1784, but during the Mexican era, seven hundred were handed out, most of them in a rush just before the American occupation.

apart the Old World. Youthful Mariano Vallejo accepted excommunication rather than give up a small library of books by freethinkers, and he and two or three other apostates nursed the forbidden doctrines of liberalism.

The contest against the central government, locally personified by the unhappy governors, vented itself in a mélange of insurrections, marches and countermarches, bloodless battles and thunderous pronunciamentos. The political issues revolved around dissatisfaction with Mexico's neglect, disposition of the evanescent treasury receipts, secularization of church property, resolution of conflicts between civil and military authority, and location of the provincial capital. For a while, the province had two capitals, one in Monterey, one in Los Angeles. The dual-headed government polarized the province into two sections, Northern and Southern California, an early manifestation of a stand that appeared off and on for the next century and still makes headlines today.

It has been fashionable to draw attention to the comic opera aspects of the revolution in California without giving credit for the solid accomplishments of the Californians and the growth of pride in their status as Californios—not Spaniards, not Mexicans —but citizens of California. When, at a later date, American troops battled them for possession of the province, some of the Yankees were surprised by the fierce resistance of these seemingly carefree people. But it was their homeland they were defending, elevated from a poverty-stricken state to a prosperous economy by their own concerted labor. Such

was the vitality of the Californio culture that it continued without change in some parts of the state for a generation after the American conquest.

In the 1840's, the burgeoning presence of Americanos in the province was becoming a progressive concern to the Californios. Early harbingers of the flood to come, a scattering of trappers, scouts, sailors, and maritime agents began to filter into the area. The first American invader to enter by an overland route, Jedediah Strong Smith, brought a ragged band of beaver trappers over the Sierra in 1828 and stayed six weeks despite official disapproval. Upon his return to the East, he published an account of his journey, which added fuel to the kindling interest in the province, served notice that an overland approach was feasible, and encouraged adventurers to take the long hike West.

The Americans who settled in the province were of two stamps: a maritime class in the coastal towns and a farming class in the inland valleys. The Yankees on the coast married into California families, became Catholics, and blended into the cultural landscape. To a man, they favored annexation of California to the United States, but by peaceful means.

The other group, following the trappers' trail, took root in the Sacramento Valley. They did not identify with the Californios or with the Americanos on the coast. They, too, favored annexation, but by direct action, Texas-style. As events were soon to prove, these two enclaves were to be instrumental in setting the stage for Old Glory.

Feudal Fiefdoms

Following the breakup of the missions, the Mexican government lavishly gave away the province to private landholders who could satisfy the governor that they could successfully raise cattle.

Under the law, the minimum grant was about six and a half square miles, the maximum eleven times this area, but property owners could acquire additional acreage by purchase or trade without official interference. Acreage of this magnitude was needed to provide adequate pasturage for the three hundred thousand animals released from mission care into private hands. Most of the ranchos in operation by the time of the American take-over were modest affairs, handled by the men in the family with only a few Indian vaqueros. Some were virtual fiefdoms, conducted on a grand scale by *gente de razón* who employed armies of Indians.

The patriarch of the northern frontier, Mariano G. Vallejo, basking in a bower of femininity (he had sixteen children, adopted eight more), was the forceful and independent lord of a hundred square miles of land north of San Francisco Bay, granted in 1834, and military commander of the buffer area between the Russians and Mexicans. One of the province's most distinguished citizens, he built a town at Sonoma, a large hacienda near Petaluma, where he directed two thousand Indian plowmen, harvesters, herders, servants, weavers, and tanners, most of whom lived in their own villages on his rancho.

A private fortress, built on a bend in the Sacramento River, served as headquarters for the imperial dream of a young Swiss immigrant, John A. Sutter. Lord of a vast domain which he named New Helvetia, Sutter employed several hundred Indians to tend his crops, herd cattle, and work in the shops within the walls. The fort was defended by cannon and a small private army. Gateway to the mountain passes to the East, it became a loadstone for Americans who crossed the Sierra.

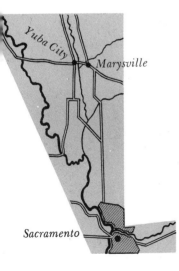

Sutter's principality, granted in 1841, stretched from Sacramento to beyond present-day Marysville; encompassed forty-eight thousand acres.

RESTLESS PASTORALE   65

The first cowboys in what is now the United States (antedating Texas by eighty years), most of the California vaqueros were Indians, trained by the padres in the rugged art of cattle raising. Although Spanish colonial policy forbade Indians from learning to ride horseback, the padres had no choice but to train hundreds of them as cowhands. The natives took to the assignment with zest, and in a short time became adept horsemen equal to any in the world.

Cattle on a Thousand Hills

The shifty and combative longhorns that plodded up the long trail from New Spain in the early days of the colony helped sustain the province in several ways. The rangy animal provided a kind of walking dry goods store, meat market, and bank.

Three-year-old steers were slaughtered whenever there was a need for food or when a trading vessel dropped anchor offshore. The animals' hides were tanned and made into rugs, blankets, curtains, sandals, chaps, saddles. Rawhide was twisted into reatas or used to lash timbers together (some mission lashings are still holding firm). Edible meat was cooked immediately, sun-dried as jerky, or pickled for barter with the trading ships. Milk, incidentally, was never drunk and was considered unhealthful. Fat was rendered into tallow and used in cooking or made into candles and soap.

Tallow in five-hundred-pound bags and the stiff dry hides, "Yankee bank notes," were the basic units of barter. Hides were processed on the shore of San Diego Bay and stored in prefabricated sheds brought from New England. Where sixty-five years before there had not been a single cow, horse, hog, sheep, or goat in all of Alta California, there were 370,000 cattle, 62,000 horses, and 320,000 sheep, hogs, and goats on the mission lands that went to the rancheros after 1834.

Every spring, while calves were still with their mothers, the rancheros took inventory of their herds. Vaqueros raced in and out of the widely scattered cattle, cutting out branded stock and assembling them within corrals for tallying and the branding of calves.

Cattle brands were designed by the rancheros themselves and registered with the authorities. Designs were mostly delightful abstractions of the initials of the owner or of the rancho.

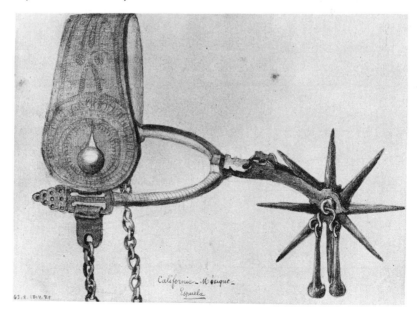

Wicked-looking spurs with five-inch rowels were worn with low-heeled boots, dragged on the ground when the vaquero dismounted, and had to be removed for walking.

RESTLESS PASTORALE 67

Trading vessels, such as the Ayacucho, usually visited the coast in pairs. The two ships would work their way up and down the shore together, remaining until their holds were tamped full of hides or all their merchandise sold to the Californios, a stay that might last a year or more. Trading voyages could net $40,000 to $65,000 a trip.

A customs seal for the port of Monterey, where officers were wont to "descend upon the ship like vultures their prey," according to the embittered captain of a Hudson's Bay Company trading vessel.

Genteel Contraband

Trading with foreign vessels, previously banned by the Spaniards, was legalized by the Mexicans, and customhouses were opened in Monterey and San Diego. Duties were high, however, and the Yankee traders adopted stratagems for evading them. They unloaded cargoes in lonely coves without benefit of customs stamp. To reduce the import taxes, ships working as a pair would transfer cargo from one to the other on the open sea, and the partially emptied ship would then make port and submit to customs inspection. Once the inventory had been taken and duties paid, it would rejoin its consort and the maneuver would be repeated in reverse. Eventually, leftover goods were smuggled ashore.

Trading vessels carried miniature department stores on board, enticing displays of gleaming copperware and pewter, jewelry, knickknacks, fine clothing, and the best furniture. To the Californios who were privileged to come aboard, the visit was an exhilarating treat. For many of the native born, it was their first view of the amenities of civilization.

In the Los Angeles area, bartered hides were brought by screeching oxcarts to the bluffs of present Dana Point and tossed to the beach below, whence they were lightered to waiting ships and taken to San Diego Bay, the Hide Capital of California, for processing in the surf.

An early photograph of a storeroom at Mission San Juan Bautista gives a hint of the range and diversity of the products acquired by the padres in exchange for hides and tallow: Peruvian vestments, a Mexican crucifix, a New England gilded mirror.

OVERLEAF: Lassoing grizzlies for bull-and-bear fights was no pastime for the fainthearted or the inexpert. Vaqueros could not risk spilling any loops on their dangerous quarry, had to ride horses trained not to panic at the scent of bear. The enraged beast was either trussed and towed back to town or, still restrained by reatas, teased into charging after one of the party who raced just ahead of its slavering jaws all the way to the plaza.

Festivals and Fandangos

Never troubled by the Puritan ethic of work for work's sake, the Californios labored only so long as it took to insure time for socializing.

Any excuse would do. A christening, wedding, feast day, wake, or any of the countless saint's days in the church calendar were ample reason to dress up in the best clothes—women in wide-flaring, bright velvets, men in bespangled gaiters and jackets—bring out the violin, guitar, the drum and cymbals, and dance away the night.

This exuberant approach to life disturbed and irritated the Yankees when they encountered it, and they looked with disfavor on a people who appeared to revel in frivolity. The Californios' delight in day-to-day living seemed sinful to the Puritans, who were more concerned with the future than the present, and later contributed to cultural conflict after the Americanos had gained the upper hand in the province.

Bloody entertainment in the plaza was sometimes provided by tethering a bull and a bear together with a chain and letting them fight to the death.

"A modern earthquake is no comparison to a California fandango, especially such as those we had in the good old times," noted Major Horace Bell, an early American resident in Los Angeles, who also observed that *"the adobe house is the best house for fandangos that ever existed—might as well try to shake down a haystack."* Unlike the baile, or private ball, the fandango was a public affair. Not every participant could afford the beautiful clothes depicted by Charles Nahl in this painting (left), nor did every fandango end up with the abduction of a fluttering maiden.

"Nothing but a tornado or a far-striking thunderbolt can overtake the Californian on horseback," wrote Walter Colton, Yankee mayor of Monterey. Racing was a favorite indulgence—even carretas raced on their way to church.

Provincial Capital

For forty years after its founding in 1771, the capital at Monterey was contained within the walls of the presidio. After Mexican independence in 1821 it began to grow as foreigners moved in and built homes outside the walls. When Richard Henry Dana visited it in 1834, he was moved to call it, "the pleasantest and most civilized looking place in California."

Eleven structures shown in the 1842
lithograph above are still standing.
Indicated at left in gray: 1. House of
Four Winds, 2. Larkin House,
3. California's first theater,
4. Customhouse, 5. Rodriques-Osio Adobe,
6. Casa Amesti, 7. Casa Alvarado,
8. Estrada Adobe, 9. Cooper-Molera
Adobe, 10. Stevenson House, 11. Royal
Presidio Chapel. Figurehead from
shoreline shipwreck, Com. Rodgers, is
drydocked at the California Historical
Society.

Yankee Take-over

Long before California became a part of the Union, it had acquired a reputation as a land of milk and honey, ineffectually ruled by a chaotic government and occupied by dilatory folk who barely scratched the natural resources everywhere at hand. Even though the land belonged to the sovereign republic of Mexico, it became of proprietary interest to Americans, who began to think of it as a proper and inevitable addition to the United States.

As more and more Yankee sea captains, trappers, fur traders, whalers, and explorers visited the province, the volume of enthusiastic reports on the undeveloped paradise began to grow, encouraging dreams of conquest.

Typical of the boosters to sing the praises of Upper California was the Yankee skipper Captain James Shaler, who visited the coast in 1803 and 1805 to take on furs. He wrote: "At great expense and considerable industry the Spaniards have removed every obstacle out of the way of an invading army; they have stocked the country with a multitude of horses, cattle, and other useful animals; . . . they have spread a number of defenceless inhabitants over the country, whom they could never induce to act as enemies to those who should treat them well; . . . in a word they have done everything that could be done to render California an object worthy of the attention of the great maritime powers . . . The conquest of this country would be absolutely nothing; it would fall without an effort to the most inconsiderable force."

Another jingoist, Thomas Jefferson Farnham, writing in the 1830's, issued a call for the right people to come to the aid of a neglected prize. "It may be confidently asserted that no country in the world possesses so fine a climate coupled with so productive a soil . . . But its miserable people live unconscious of these things. In their gardens grow the apple, the pear, the olive, fig, and orange, the Irish and sweet potato, yam and plantain most luxuriantly, side by side; and yet they sleep, and smoke and hum some tune of Castilian laziness, while surrounding Nature is thus inviting them to the noblest and richest rewards of honorable toil."

Appeals such as these, appearing in government publications, newspapers, and books, stirred hundreds of restless souls to turn westward beyond the frontier and strike out for the Promised Land.

Official Washington was acutely aware of the rich prize waiting on the Pacific Coast, and negotiations for the purchase of California were started early in the 1800's under President Andrew Jackson. The President sent an emissary to Mexico City empowered to purchase California and New Mexico for five hundred thousand dollars. Negotiations dragged on for six years without result. The succession of Mexican presidents was too insecure in their tenure to risk the suicidal sale of California to the gringos—much as they would have dearly loved to take the proffered money.

Under successive administrations in Washington, other attempts at acquisition were advanced. Some

Hero or villain? Filibusterer or trusted emissary? Whatever his motives, John Charles Frémont did more than any other man to precipitate the seizure of California. Flamboyant in all his actions, he is here portrayed in later life amid the trappings of an artillery post.

Manifest destiny: At the time the Spanish colony was founded in California, it was comfortably separated by the width of an entire continent from the colonies of Spain's hated imperial rival, Great Britain. Within eighty years, the successors to Britain's empire would conquer the successors to Spain's and extend the western boundary of an aggressive young nation to the Pacific Coast.

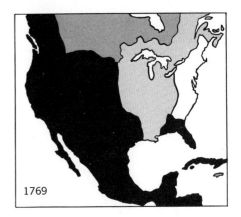

1769

involved the combination of California and Texas in a single package, some linked California with Oregon; one proposal called for purchase of San Francisco Bay. The stakes increased with each new offer, reaching an ultimate high of forty million dollars.

The President who ultimately effected the conquest of California, James K. Polk, entered office in 1845 with a pledge to take California by any means. With approval of his cabinet, he instituted a three-pronged offensive. He dispatched a negotiator to Mexico City to attempt outright purchase; his second line of attack was to encourage the establishment of an independent California under an American protectorate; and, failing both alternatives, he was ready to go to war as a last resort.

The first plan failed, partly because of the blundering of a naval squadron that had prematurely seized Monterey three years earlier, an act that had made the Mexicans wary of the United States' intentions. The second plan was well on its way to fulfillment under the direction of Polk's designated agent in California, Thomas O. Larkin, United States Consul in Monterey. With full authority from the President, Larkin recruited leading Californians to the cause of independence and pledged American protection for the proposed colony. Unhappily, this scheme went glimmering when a group of disgruntled Americans took matters into their own rough hands and declared an independent republic in 1846.

Polk's determination to seize California was abetted by the knowledge that England was likewise bent on a course of conquest. British emissaries in Mexico City were busy trying to effect an agreement for the absorption of California into the British empire, and agents in London were laboring to commit their government into taking aggressive

steps. At the time, London was reluctant to expand its holdings, especially at the risk of head-on confrontation with the United States, so the moves were cautious and dilatory.

Nevertheless, considerable British activity was taking place. English subjects living in the province began proselytizing for a British protectorate. A special colonizing venture was approved by the Mexican government in 1846 that would have established a large Irish settlement in Northern California. Fur brigades of the Hudson's Bay Company had trapped in the Siskiyous and Sacramento Valley from 1826 on, and a trading store was opened in Yerba Buena in 1841. Sir George Simpson, governor of the company, wrote in 1842, "the principal people in the country and indeed the whole population seem anxious to be released from the Republic of Mexico . . . I have reason to believe they would require very little encouragement to declare their independence of Mexico and place themselves under the protection of Great Britain."

The British had good reason to be optimistic about the Mexicans' enthusiasm for a British takeover because the republic was indebted twenty-six million dollars to British financial interests, and the debt could easily be liquidated by exchanging California for the defaulted bonds. British warships were poised off the Mexican coast, stalking an American squadron that was awaiting orders to sail to California.

Relations between the United States and Mexico deteriorated steadily and erupted into war in May 1846 after a series of incidents along the Rio Grande. Although California was not a cause of the war, its fate became involved with the general conflagration, and military action was begun as soon as word of a state of war reached the naval and land forces waiting outside the California

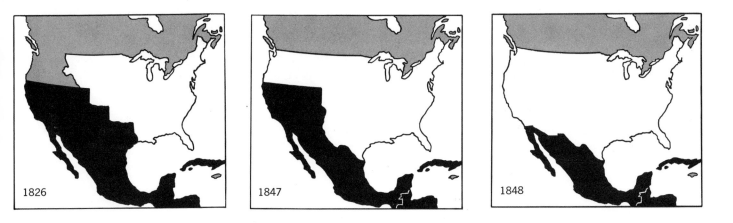

1826   1847   1848

boundaries. Commodore Sloat landed marines in Monterey on July 7, 1846, and hoisted the Stars and Stripes. Two days later, the colors were raised in San Francisco by Captain John Montgomery (for whom the "Wall Street of the West" was subsequently named); a few weeks later the flag flew over San Diego and Los Angeles.

Two days after the seizure of Monterey, the British admiral sailed into port, ready to take advantage of the confusion, only to find that the United States had the province already firmly within its grip.

Actual hostilities in California had started before war was declared. A group of American malcontents living in the Sacramento Valley rebelled against the Mexican authorities June 14 and proclaimed an independent nation, popularly known as the Bear Flag Republic. Masking what was really an act of aggression, the insurgents justified their actions in a high-sounding proclamation issued in Sonoma that announced the formation of the Republic of California, "which shall secure to all civil and religious liberty; which shall detect and punish crime; which shall encourage industry, virtue and literature; which shall leave unshackled by Fetters, Commerce, Agriculture, and Mechanism."

The pronouncement promised a government that would be "prosperous and happifying in its tendency."

The spread-eagle language cloaked a movement of obscure intent. The rebels captured prominent Northern Californians, including Mariano Vallejo, commandant of the northern frontier, and imprisoned them in Sutter's Fort for several weeks. The rebels turned their cause over to Captain John Charles Frémont, then loitering in the area under mystifying circumstances, and he formed them into an undisciplined army. When Monterey was of-

ficially seized by naval forces three weeks later, July 7, 1846, the Bear Flag Republic was dissolved and the Bear Flaggers were absorbed into the Army as the California Volunteers under Frémont.

He had arrived in the province late in 1845 on the second of several exploring expeditions into the West. The presence of his heavily armed "topographical engineers" aroused suspicion and resentment, and when he directed his motley band in acts of belligerency, he forced the Californians to take arms against him and caused Thomas Larkin to request his recall because of the damage that he was inflicting on the cause of peaceful acquisition.

Following the Bear Flag rebellion, which was generally credited to Frémont's machinations, he commanded an army of ruffians who subdued Mexican resistance in Northern California and then marched south to assist the beleaguered American forces in Los Angeles.

Although the war did not last long, the reduction of California was delayed by American blundering in Southern California. At the start, the Californians were too preoccupied preparing for a civil war among themselves to contest the initial forays of the American troops. Opposition was sporadic and easily overcome by American forces, and within a month it appeared that California had been won with hardly any bloodshed. Such a conclusion proved premature, however, when inept handling of the pueblo of Los Angeles provoked a brave and spirited defense that delayed occupation of the land for four months. Repulsed, the American troops regrouped for a successful assault on Los Angeles, the final holdout of the Californians. Frémont's battalion, marching down from the conquered north, met the remaining Mexican forces at Cahuenga Pass and negotiated the capitulation that ended the campaign in California.

European Toeholds

The United States was not the only country with covetous designs on California. Efforts were being made in England to bring the province into the empire, but the most formidable competitor was czarist Russia, which had a solid footing on the provincial soil north of Bodega.

The colony, which had been established with the tacit approval of the Spaniards in 1812, had proved inadequate to support the starving colonists in Alaska, and the czar in 1822 ordered further expansion southward along the coast and down into Baja, if necessary. Powerless to resist this intrusion, the Mexican authorities would doubtless have condoned it, but in 1823 the American government, though no party to the controversy, issued President Monroe's famous doctrine forbidding further European expansion. Rather than face war with the United States, the Russians abandoned their plans and soon dissolved the colony as well, selling it off lock, stock, and gun barrel to John Sutter.

Mercantile representative of Great Britain, the Hudson's Bay Company was very active in the province from 1826–46. Headquarters in Yerba Buena, at the corner of Montgomery and Clay streets, served for five years, 1841–46. The company's ships stopped here to exchange goods for hides and tallow, grain, and furs.

Though a disappointment to its sponsors, Fort Ross (1812–39) was a busy place
in its heyday. Eighty-five buildings, mostly within the stockade, sheltered 150
Russian-Aleuts, who tilled fields, tended cattle, and hunted sea otter. The Russians
built five ships in a yard at the base of the cliffs and prefabricated several cabins,
which they shipped to Alaska.

Visitors to the fort reported the trappings
of civilization: excellent food and wines,
Mozart concerts, and petit point, such
as this sampler, which translates: "To be
merry is the nature of the Russians,
through all the length and breadth of
their native land."

A delightful sketch in the journal of Gunner William Meyers shows the American Marines seizing the undefended fort at Monterey in 1842. Commodore Jones found no evidence that the two countries were at war, and discreetly retreated. The Mexican governor, then on his way to Los Angeles, blustered, "I wished myself a thunderbolt to fly and intimidate the invaders, but 110 leagues intervened between them and me and my forces were all infantry." He later pressed an indemnity claim against Jones for 1500 complete military uniforms and "a complete set of military musical instruments to replace those ruined" on the forced march to Monterey to repel the premature invasion.

Anticipating Old Glory

Negotiations for the purchase of California for forty million dollars, though never very promising, received a setback when American naval forces jumped the gun and seized Monterey in 1842 under the impression that the United States and Mexico were at war and that the latter country intended to cede California to Great Britain. The landing party found the province at peace and withdrew with apologies, but the misadventure soured negotiations.

Seemingly more propitious was the scheme to encourage local leaders in establishing an independent state, free of Mexico. Thomas O. Larkin, United States consul in Monterey, received secret instructions in 1845 to promote peaceful separation. He informed important Californians that the United States would not foment revolution but would protect any group that sought to sever from Mexico and that his country would prevent cession of California to a European power. The plan was progressing well and was within a year or two from fruition when it was blocked by the Bear Flag rebellion.

A key figure in preparing the way for peaceful occupation of California, Thomas Larkin established himself in Monterey in 1832 and directed several flourishing businesses before entering political life. His beautiful home, sporting an interior staircase, combines New England, plantation, and Spanish architectural styles in a form that has been known ever since as the "Monterey style."

Headed for Mexican California in 1846, the ill-fated Donner Party became trapped in deep snow in the Sierra. Of the seventy-nine who started over the mountains, only forty-five lived, some resorting to cannibalism to survive.

Coming of the Americanos

No matter that California was Mexican territory officially off limits to Americans, thousands of immigrants crossed the Sierra in the 1840's, confident that they would find acceptance in the new land.

Differing significantly from the solitary trappers and sailors who had preceded them, the newcomers came in organized parties equipped with wagons, livestock, and household gear. Unlike their forerunners who had melded into Mexican society, the colonists remained aloof, squatted on Mexican land, and raised crops and grazed cattle in competition with the Californians. They felt no allegiance to Mexico and no respect for Mexican law. Their rooted presence distressed provincial authorities, and the governor issued a proclamation banning American immigration. He jailed and deported a few unruly Yankees, but he was helpless to stem the steadily growing tide.

Absence of roads did not deter immigrants who brought wagons across anyhow after 1844, winched them up steep slopes (as in the sketch), or took them apart and lowered them down precipices.

The Promised Land *is the fitting title bestowed by the artist on this painting of a pioneer settler with his wife and child as they look out over the lush valleys spread below them this bright day in 1846. The terrors of the desert and the mountain crossing are behind them, and they can relax in the glowing promise of the future. This emotional moment affected every party that crossed the Sierra, when they first sighted the land which was to be their home.*

War Starts in the North

Failing by negotiation and guile to acquire California, Washington was ready with the final alternative: war.

American military forces were poised in the wings awaiting their cues, and as soon as war broke out along the Rio Grande, word was dispatched to California, and the waiting forces took possession.

Hostilities got a head start in Sonoma, where a group of dissident Americans seized Mexican authorities and proclaimed the Republic of California, hopefully modeled on the Lone Star Republic of Texas. The revolt was taken over by John Charles Frémont and his band of unsavory "topographical engineers." He absorbed the Bear Flaggers into his command, swore them into the U. S. Army, and marched on Monterey, where they joined forces with naval units. Campaigning in Northern California was quickly concluded.

The Bear Flag borrowed star and bar from the United States flag, added a grizzly which has been faulted as "more porcine and lupine than ursine in configuration."

Without firing a shot, forces from the U. S. Pacific Squadron disembarked at Monterey July 7, 1846, and raised the Stars and Stripes at the customhouse. Commodore Sloat issued a conciliatory proclamation that granted full rights to all Californians and promised riches to everyone from the forthcoming affiliation with the United States.

Frémont leads a ragged column of Americanos toward Monterey after the defeat of California lancers in the Battle of Navidad near San Juan Bautista.

The Battle of San Gabriel River effectively ended the war in California on January 8, 1847. The Californians, attempting to prevent American troops from fording the river, were driven off. A second skirmish, the next day, ended inconclusively, but on the third day U.S. forces reoccupied Los Angeles.

Military Stand-off in the South

The reduction of California took a very different course in Southern California from the easy conquest of the north. Thanks to inept American military leadership and unexpectedly spirited resistance by the Californians, the American troops were held at bay for four months and ignominiously forced to retreat.

American infantrymen occupied the pueblo of Los Angeles August 18, 1846, taking positions on a height overlooking the town. Unfortunately, they were left in the charge of a martinet who imposed such harsh controls over the residents that the Angelenos rebelled and drove the Americans out of the city and down to the waterfront.

As further insult, the Californians inflicted a smashing military defeat on a column of dragoons, grandiloquently known as the Army of the West, which was on its way to join the naval forces supposedly in possession of California.

In due time, the Americans co-ordinated their forces and met the Californians in a confrontation that ended in the Americans' favor. Terms of capitulation were signed soon after.

ADVERSARIES: *The dashing commander of the California lancers who defeated the Army of the West, General Andrés Pico was later designated to sign terms of capitulation. The no-nonsense commander of the American forces, Commodore Robert F. Stockton, had fought in the War of 1812. After the war with Mexico, he resigned from the Navy, served in the U. S. Senate, then went into business in the East.*

A smashing defeat for the U. S. Army at San Pasqual was brought about by superior knowledge of the terrain and superb horsemanship on the part of the California lancers under General Pico. The Americans lost thirty-six men—eighteen killed, eighteen wounded, including the commanding officer—in the fifteen-minute conflict, and they were forced to stay in a fortified camp until rescue forces could reach them from San Diego.

Much as they disliked Frémont, the Californians nevertheless chose to surrender to him rather than to the other military authorities in the area. Frémont signed the capitulation agreement with General Andrés Pico on January 13, 1847, at Cahuenga.

Prize of War

With the campaign for California concluded, the war with Mexico dragged on for a few more weeks, and then it too sputtered to an end. California's war ended with the capitulation of General Andrés Pico in 1847; the main war ended with the Treaty of Guadalupe Hidalgo, signed February 2, 1848.

The treaty was a generous one—promising all things to all men. It was drawn up with high resolve, promising that no one would be penalized for having fought against the Americans, that all property rights would be respected, and all citizens of the former province would automatically become American subjects unless they chose otherwise. As treaties go, it was a good one. Unfortunately, the United States never did quite live up to its high-sounding clauses.

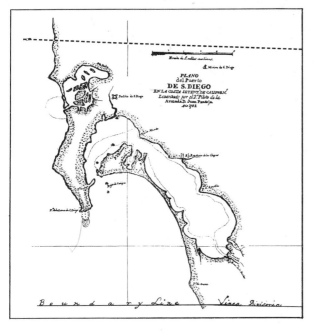

Postponed for two hectic years, California's admission as a state, when finally approved by Congress on September 9, 1850, touched off wild celebrations throughout the thirty-first state. So enthusiastically was the news received that the day was made a legal holiday and has been celebrated ever since.

In the Treaty of Guadalupe Hidalgo, which ended the war between Mexico and the United States, it was almost by a fluke that San Diego turned up on the American instead of the Mexican side of the border. Mexican negotiators pressed hard for a boundary north of the port (indicated by dashed line) on the grounds that they needed the harbor, but American bargainers held out and shrewdly won the day. Today's boundary line is seen at the bottom of the map.

1848-1854

Gold Fever

THE year 1848 opened quietly enough. The war in California had been over for a year, and though peace negotiations still dragged on, no one doubted the outcome of the treaty. California was firmly attached to the United States, and a provisional military government was keeping things in check.

Geographically and politically California was even farther from the center of power in Washington than it had been from Mexico City. Separated from Eastern centers of commerce by desert and mountain barriers, and by eighteen thousand miles of ocean, it was in truth a remote island. At the slow pace of Americanization, California seemed destined to require a decade or more to catch up with the rest of the country.

This was the setting when 1848 opened. By the time this pivotal year had drawn to a close, the picture was explosively different. The languid land, Mexican-dominated along the coast and Indian territory inland, would find itself catapulted into the front ranks of history. Within a few months, one of the greatest migrations since the Crusades would converge on the state, tear its foothills apart, build cities where none had existed before, and overwhelm Indian and Mexican alike with an alien culture.

The catalyst, of course, was the discovery of gold by James Marshall on January 24, 1848.

The tale is a familiar one. Marshall had recently

Negro and white miners work a Long Tom near Auburn in 1852. Hundreds of Negroes came to the gold region and worked as independent miners. Some of them earned enough in the diggings to buy freedom for themselves and their families.

crossed the Sierra with a colonizing party. A carpenter by trade, he was hired by John Sutter to build a sawmill at Coloma, forty miles to the north of Sutter's Fort and within the dominion of New Helvetia. It was here that Marshall sighted the gold nugget that turned the world upside down.

He wrapped the nugget in his handkerchief and took it to the fort to show his boss. Behind locked doors the two men tested the metal and satisfied themselves that it was real gold. Sutter swore Marshall to secrecy for six weeks, hoping by the end of that time to have his crops harvested before his farmhands would vanish in quest of gold. Perhaps he had a premonition of the turmoil that the discovery would ignite. As events soon proved, the secret was too tantalizing to be kept, the news leaked out, and in time Sutter was fated to lose everything in the social cataclysm that followed.

This was not the first time that gold had been discovered in California. Six years earlier, in March of 1842, gold nuggets had been found by a mission Indian while he was gathering wild onions on the lands of San Gabriel Mission. The discovery touched off a minor gold rush in Southern California and attracted prospectors from Sonora, Mexico. The first gold shipment from California was sent from Los Angeles to the United States Mint in Philadelphia by Don Abel Stearns on September 22, 1842, and regularly thereafter for several years. However, the Mexican government did not exploit the discovery.

As a matter of fact, Marshall's discovery likewise attracted little notice at first. The newspaper mentioned it casually. Few readers took the word seriously, and some even suspected that it was a ruse, a "Yankee invention, got up to reconcile the people to the change of flag." At length, a few curious souls went off to see for themselves, and when they returned with dust, others followed. Those who reached the mountains in 1848 found a seemingly inexhaustible supply of gold in gravel beds, potholes, stream channels, and sand bars where it had accumulated unnoticed for centuries. As the news spread, every able-bodied man headed for the diggings.

Wrote Walter Alton, *alcalde* of Monterey: "The blacksmith dropped his hammer, the carpenter his plane, the mason his trowel, the farmer his sickle, the baker his loaf, and the tapster his bottle. All were off for the mines, some on horses, some on carts, some on crutches, and one went in a litter."

The rush of 1848 was strictly local. Except for a large group from Sonora, Mexico, the miners came almost entirely from within the state. News of the bonanza was quickly spread beyond the borders by word of mouth, letters, newspaper reports, government bulletins. The story was skeptically received until President James K. Polk unequivocally informed Congress: "The accounts of the abundance of gold in that territory are of such an extraordinary character as would scarcely command belief were they not corroborated by authentic reports of officers in the public service." With an official seal placed on the news, the nation became delirious with gold fever.

The timing could not have been more fortuitous. The doctrine of manifest destiny had already fired the enthusiasm of Americans to continue the westward march to the Pacific, and thousands were poised to leave for the far frontier with the coming of spring. News of the gold discovery burst the dam.

First to leave were those along the eastern seaboard who engaged passage on the first ships they could board and headed around the Horn on a six-month voyage, or across the Isthmus of Panama in what could be a month's trip. So frantic was the rush that every kind of vessel, trustworthy or not, was hastily readied for passengers and put to sea. Scores of leaky boats with hundreds of gold seekers were never heard from again, victims of poor seamanship, storms, or foundering.

To the gold seekers in the Midwest, the logical route was overland. Unlike their counterparts on the East Coast, they could not leave any time they wished. They had to wait until spring, when the forage grass was tall enough to sustain pack animals, and they could not depart too late in the year lest they be snowbound in the Sierra passes.

The electrifying news started a tide of gold seekers throughout the world. Chileans were the first to learn of the discovery when California-bound vessels stopped in Valparaíso for supplies. The Chileans embarked by the hundreds, settling in San Francisco and the southern mines. The news reached Europeans suffering a depression and crop failure. Ireland had just passed through disastrous potato famines. Europeans migrated by the thousands, settling in colonies throughout the lode. From around the Pacific came Kanakas, Chinese, and the odious Sydney Ducks from Australia, which was still a penal colony.

As foreigners continued to arrive, their growing numbers stirred resentment. They tended to band together and did not mix with the Americans, who mistrusted their strange dress and barbarous languages. By 1850, they comprised a quarter of the population, and within a decade, nearly 40 per cent of the state was foreign-born.

Fear that aliens would carry away more than their share of gold prompted the Americans to initiate repressive measures. A foreign miners' tax, introduced in 1850, forced many to return home. In the diggings, vigilante groups evicted colonies of Mexicans, Chileans, and French from their claims and homes. The oppressive treatment generated ill-will among the foreign-born and also set a sorry precedent for future discriminatory actions that have periodically wracked California politics.

The forty-niners fanned out over the foothills, quickly exhausting the easy pickings in the lowland stream beds, and settled wherever there was news of gold, moving restlessly from one strike to another in quest of the bonanza. The thousands who covered the foothills tore apart the existing life of the area. The Yankees drove out the Indians, shooting them if they resisted (no man could even be tried for shooting an Indian).

Next to feel the invasion were the Californios and the first American settlers. Some miners helped themselves to livestock and horses, cut down orchards for firewood, and squatted on land belonging to others or sold it without title to the next man. Sutter's Fort, in the path of swarms of ior ARROW ROOT and 500 lbs. COCOA, recommended by the faculty, well worthy the attention of Invalids, &c.

GOLD MINE FOUND.—In the newly made raceway of the Saw Mill recently erected by Captain Sutter, on the American Fork, gold has been found in considerable quantities. One person brought thirty dollars worth to New Helvetia, gathered there in a short time. California, no doubt, is rich in mineral wealth; great chances here for scientific capitalists. Gold has been found in almost every part of the country.

AUTOGRAPH OF

Jas. W. Marshall.

OLD SUTTER MILL.

THE DISCOVERER OF GOLD IN CALIFORNIA

January 19th. 1848

Announcement of the discovery of gold barely made the front page of a San Francisco newspaper (left)—but soon after, the paper shut down while editor and staff went off to the diggings. Subsequently, Marshall's role as discoverer was questioned by doubters and he issued autographed cards (above) to reinforce his claim to this momentous happenstance.

human locusts, was swept under. By 1851 Sutter was nearly bankrupt and he retired to a farm near Marysville. But even here he was ousted by forty-niners and sent on his way, ultimately to die almost penniless in Washington, where he had gone to seek reimbursement from Congress for his losses.

A rambunctious, hard-drinking, and hard-living lot, the young miners led a toilsome life, most of them on the edge of hardship and privation. Robberies, murders, and hangings were not uncommon; and the shanty towns were frequently wiped out by fire. Without courts or laws, the polyglot group nevertheless managed to conduct their affairs with surprising comradery. Relying on common sense, the Bible, or laws from back home, they improvised a society of astonishing cohesiveness. Lynch law took over once in a while, but on the whole, claims were adjusted, misdeeds punished, and business conducted with a minimum of confusion.

In much of the rest of the state, life continued as before. From Monterey southward cattle grazed unrestrictedly on the ranchos, and the rancheros became wealthy from the sudden demand for beef, needed to feed the hungry miners. Rancheros spent their new wealth on fine clothes, silver harnesses, and social activities. They paid a dear price for this profligacy later, but for a long time they lived off the fat of the land.

The great rush petered out as rapidly as it had built up. Thousands of disillusioned miners returned home, glad to escape from the hard toil and poor pay in the hot gold fields, lucky to leave with their lives and their health. The mining of gold had become big business as the ore became increasingly difficult to remove, and its extraction took capital and corporate organization.

Of the gold mined in California, very little remained to enrich the new state. Billions of dollars were taken out each year, but most of it went East or to Europe to repay loans made to gold-mining companies. The unprecedented volume of gold flooded world markets and depressed the economies of several countries. Some of the gold helped finance the Union side of the Civil War, some leaked into Confederate hands.

The new state found itself immeasurably enriched in other ways, however. The Gold Rush had compressed a half century of normal growth into a half decade, and when it was over, the state's population had quadrupled, a dozen new cities flourished where none had existed before, and the mud flats of Yerba Buena had been transformed into a world port. Schools, libraries, and churches began to appear, reassuring evidence of social and cultural growth. The cosmopolitan character of the new pioneers contributed the heritage of a dozen countries to the economic, social, and cultural development of the state.

The Rush by Land

Thousands hiked or rode the 1800-mile overland trail to California from the Midwest. The journey took six months—about the same time as the all-ocean route. So many came overland that by August 1850 forty-five thousand gold seekers (including five thousand women and children) had passed through Fort Laramie. An equal number followed other routes.

Death, disease, and starvation dogged the weary parties. Asiatic cholera killed five thousand men en route in 1849, and hundreds succumbed to mountain fever, diarrhea, and other disorders. Scurvy waited for many of the survivors after they reached California. The six-month journey without an adequate intake of Vitamin C made many of the Argonauts susceptible to the disability that had long been considered a maritime monopoly, the ancient curse of the long sea voyage.

The journey was an ordeal that few would forget. The journals of the overland parties, which far outnumber the bored writings of the sea voyagers, tell over and over of the land's immensity, the hardships, and unexpected rewards of the exhausting trip.

{ Carcass which the author subsisted upon, from 22ᵈ Decʳ

The descent to the Green River was just one of the hazards of the overland ordeal. Mules, wagons, and teamsters slid down the slope. The wheel mules sat on their haunches, "with heads up & fore feet straight to the front & close together to resist the pressure behind." The Green was a welcome oasis for the animals and men who had just crossed fifty miles of waterless desert.

The overlanders left a wake of abandoned equipment, spoiled food, broken wagons, and dead animals. Graves marked every mile.

(straggling emigrants are passing)

Above the grave of the Alfor is shown on the hill, below which are seen the dispositions their camp, and the fatal Oak.

The long voyage was a blur of rough weather, seasickness, overcrowding, poor food, and endless boredom.

The Rush by Sea

Word of the California discovery swept to the far corners of the globe, and gold-hungry men embarked in whatever vessels would get them to San Francisco.

From the East Coast, the safest, if most tedious, route was around the Horn, following the wake of the early Boston traders. The voyage could take as long as nine months if adverse weather were encountered. The Argonauts landed in California soft from the enforced rest, many of them ill-prepared for the arduous physical labor that awaited them in the mines.

The more impatient elected to cross the Isthmus of Panama with the hope of saving precious time. With luck, a New Yorker could reach San Francisco in four weeks by this route—providing he did not come down with malaria or cool his heels in Panama City for several weeks waiting for a steamer. At one time, there were three thousand men waiting for passage north on the overburdened vessels.

Some lazy gold seekers hired porters to carry them across the Isthmus piggyback.

Forty-niners who chose the Isthmus short cut endured hardships and risked jungle fever, cholera, and death. For the first stage, they were poled up the crocodile-infested Chagres River in small boats to the headwater, where they transferred to mule train for a steamy fifty-mile hike over the mountains to Panama.

Gold fever drew thousands from Great Britain, Ireland, Germany, and France. Guides to the gold region (below) were published in Germany. French mining companies brought in four thousand miners. By 1852, San Francisco was said to be half Irish.

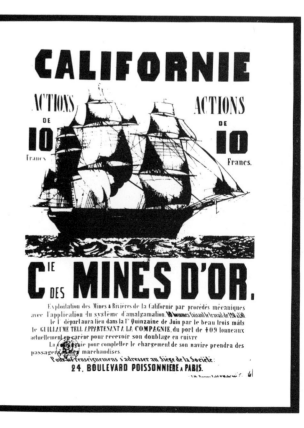

Vessels that brought the forty-niners were abandoned by crews and captains alike as soon as they dropped anchor in San Francisco Bay. At one time, five hundred ships lay rotting in the bay mud, their crews gone, no one on hand to unload the spoiling cargoes. A water-borne city grew up among the stranded hulks, which were connected by catwalks.

Instant Metropolis

During 1848, San Francisco welcomed a total of two ships. But in the following year, 775 cleared from New York alone and more than thirty-two thousand passengers sailed through the Golden Gate. In the last six months of 1849, twenty-four thousand men landed—and five hundred women, most of whom were up to no good.

The tide of newcomers quickly transformed the town into a brawling city. Blocks were laid out, houses, churches, and schools built, and plank sidewalks laid to keep pedestrians from vanishing in the muddy streets. Along with such civic betterments there also grew a vigorous sporting life, supported by five hundred saloons, forty-six gambling parlors, and forty-eight bawdyhouses.

The shallow harbor, inadequate for the maritime commerce that overwhelmed it, sprouted wharves and ramshackle improvements. Dismasted ships were hauled onto the mud flats to serve as business buildings. As the port expanded into the bay, the land-locked vessels were sunk and became part of the bay fill. Their bones still rest under lower Market Street and the financial district.

In the absence of hotels, forty-niners improvised tent communities from the sails of marooned ships. One crowned Telegraph Hill in 1849–50.

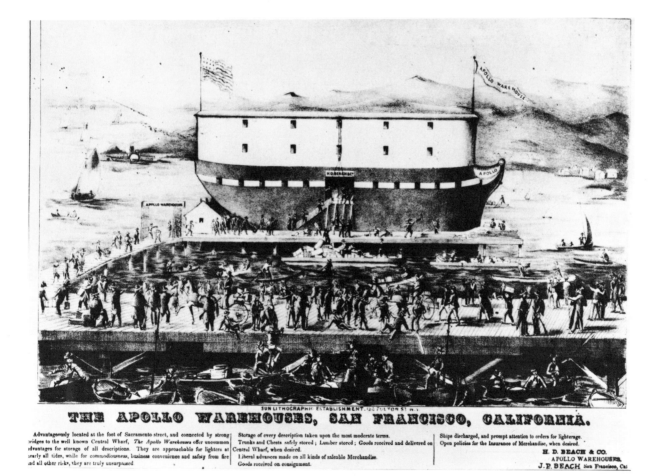

THE APOLLO WAREHOUSES, SAN FRANCISCO, CALIFORNIA.

Advantageously located at the foot of Sacramento street, and connected by strong bridges to the well known Central Wharf, The Apollo Warehouses offer uncommon advantages for storage of all descriptions. They are approachable for lighters at nearly all tides, while for commodiousness, business convenience and safety from fire and all other risks, they are truly unsurpassed.

Storage of every description taken upon the most moderate terms. Trunks and Chests safely stored; Lumber stored; Goods received and delivered on Central Wharf, when desired. Liberal advances made on all kinds of saleable Merchandise. Goods received on consignment.

Ships discharged, and prompt attention to orders for lighterage. Open policies for the Insurance of Merchandise, when desired.

H. D. BEACH & CO.
APOLLO WAREHOUSES.
J. P. BEACH San Francisco, Cal

The quickest way to acquire a building was to commandeer an abandoned ship, such as the Apollo, *here reincarnated as a warehouse. Other ships served as hotels, restaurants, a jail, and an insane asylum.*

GOLD FEVER   101

Mining Towns

Canvas mining encampments blossomed like spring weeds wherever the diggings showed promise, and vanished when the gold petered out. Many were christened with raffish names as temporary as the towns themselves: Delirium Tremens, Gomorrah, Humbug, Jackass Hill, You Bet, Bedbug.

Settlements near the rich deposits achieved a precarious permanence, ever threatened by failure of the water supply, depletion of the gold, or by conflagration. The tinder-dry towns were only one spark away from obliteration. Heated and lighted by open flame, the towns were lucky to pass through a boisterous weekend without going up in smoke. The firehouse was as imposing as the village church or city hall, and the volunteer firemen were considered among the privileged elite.

Merchants wearied of replacing burned-out stores every few weeks and began rebuilding with stone, metal roofing, and steel shutters, which gave some fire protection and a permanence beyond the town's own lifespan.

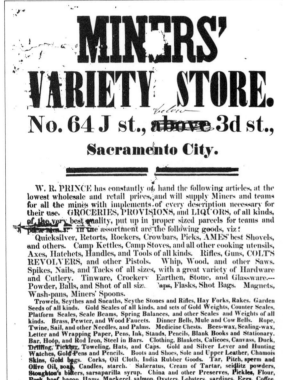

Storekeepers stocked a conglomeration of goods for the miners' work, protection, nourishment, and amusement.

The hilly town of Sonora, named for the home province of the Mexican miners who settled there in 1848, was nearly depopulated by an outbreak of scurvy that afflicted half the residents. A special hospital was built to treat the sick with lime juice and raw potatoes. In 1850, the pioneering Sonorans were driven out by vigilantes who disliked sharing the natural wealth with aliens.

Added to the perils of fire and storm, the periodic danger of flooding kept life eventful in lowland river towns. Sacramentans often had to take to rowboats when runoffs filled their streets.

Life in the Diggings

For the bearded youngsters from all over the world, life in the diggings was no vacation outing. Digging gold out of river beds was hot, backbreaking work in summer, and chilly, ague-inducing torment in winter. To make his beans, a placer miner had to shovel at least a ton of gravel a day. Although the miners' incomes averaged above their previous wages as tradesmen, farm hands, and day laborers, their profits were erased by the exorbitant costs of necessities. With butter at six dollars a pound, boots fifty dollars a pair, and blankets fifty to a hundred dollars, the miners' dust vanished into the merchants' pokes.

The arduous nature of the work and constant exposure to wet and cold made for susceptibility to a variety of illnesses, usually self-doctored with nostrums. The monotonous diet of beans and bacon induced scurvy among scores of miners, many of whom died in Sonora and Drytown.

For recreation, the lusty young men turned to the traditional saloon, gambling parlor, and pleasure house.

The popular painting Sunday Morning in the Mines, *by the contemporary artist Charles Nahl, squeezes almost every aspect of the miners' free time into a single canvas. This romantic view shows high-spirited youths fighting, racing, gambling, and dancing, while a dutiful few write home, read the Bible, wash long johns or contemplate the passing show. The actuality was far more drab, but this was the way the miners wanted to remember it.*

A French salad plate carries a scene from a popular serial about the misadventures of two Frenchmen in the gold fields. One of the hapless miners, on his way to town with his strike, is shown confronted by desperadoes—a far-from-fictional likelihood in the gold region. The French people, caught in a severe depression, avidly followed doings in the gold region reported in volume by their press.

Poignant evidence of the youthfulness of the forty-niners is carved into the headstones in the old cemeteries. Far from home, the young men died alone, sometimes violently, usually without medical aid. Cholera, pneumonia, scurvy, consumption, accidents, and murder accounted for most of the deaths.

JACOB R. GIDDIS
Aged
28 Yrs.
Murdered on or
About the 28th
Day of June 1861.

IN
memory of
JOHN L. GREGG
Formely of Elyria
Ohio Died Septr.
15th 1855.
In the 25th year
of his Age.

MARY E.
wife of
J. Hummell
Died
Oct. 24. 1850
Aged 16 Yrs.
4 mo. & 4 days
Heaven is our home

J. HUMMELL
Died
Nov 9. 1851
Aged
23 years

OVERLEAF: *Supply wagons carried equipment and food to miners in remote diggings, brought back gold dust to be refined. The difficulty of transporting goods long distances over poor roads to the scattered population kept costs high.*

Mining Techniques

Basic gold-mining techniques used in California were imported from foreign lands. Placer-mining methods were brought by the Sonorans who migrated from northern Mexico in 1848. Drawing on long experience, they taught the Yankee clerks, bankers, and soldiers turned miners how to manipulate a pan, cradle, long tom, or sluice box, and they introduced the mule-powered arrastra for pulverizing ore. When the surface deposits had been depleted and it became necessary to dig deep into the mountains, it was the hard-rock miners from Wales and Cornwall who showed how it should be done.

Whatever the method, a volume flow of running water was an essential element. The first diggings were all located along rivers, but these soon became overcrowded and the miners turned to the dry beds of seasonal streams or ancient rivers and imported water via long flumes. By 1859, nearly six thousand miles of flumes and pipe lines festooned the gold country.

Ingenious miners turned aside rivers to expose the gold deposited in the stream bed. The operation took capital, a large amount of co-operative labor—and fast work, lest a sudden rise in the river wipe out all the effort. Here, the stream has been dammed, diverted into a flume, and power taken from it by water wheels to operate mining machinery.

Large-scale mining operations were cluttered with Rube Goldbergian machinery improvised to extract the gold. If the diggings were near a town, they were visited on Sundays by townsfolk who came out to gossip, cadge souvenir nuggets, and get their pictures taken by an itinerant daguerreotypist.

Methods for reclaiming gold relied on fact that it is heavier than other metals, and when gold-laden gravel is suspended in water, the heavy metal will fall to the bottom and the light particles wash away. Miles of wooden flumes carried water to otherwise dry diggings. A contemporary drawing shows miners using pans, cradles, long toms, and flumes while hard-rock miners tunnel into a hillside.

Hydraulicking

The ultimate development in extractive technology, the hydraulic monitors washed away whole mountains and sent the mud cascading through sluices

where the gold was removed. Pioneered in 1852, they were finally turned off by court action in the 1880's because of damage to crops and rivers in the Central Valley.

"As Sweet as the music of Children's Laughter
As Pure as the heart of a little Child."

GHIRARDELLI'S GROUND CHOCOLATE

GEO. C. SHREVE & CO.

Of the hundreds of firms that were started during the Gold Rush (1849–54), 150 are still thriving today. Mostly local or statewide businesses, a few have earned national reputations and their trade names, such as the five on this page, are widely known. Oldest of these are Shreve and Levi Strauss, which date from 1850. The three other firms were founded in 1852. There are still twenty-two firms in Northern California that date from 1849, including the prestigious Ritz Old Poodle Dog and the Tadich Grill.

Perhaps best known of the Gold Rush firms is the ubiquitous Wells Fargo, long identified with the Gold Rush and the West by viewers of television. The company started as an express service (1852), branched out into banking, and later covered the West with a network of stage lines.

Commercial Heritage

When the Gold Rush ended in 1854 or so, the state slumped into a depression. Unemployed miners gravitated to the cities, businesses that had catered to them failed, and overcommitted banks closed their doors.

The army of men gradually dispersed. Many returned home, some sought new El Dorados in other states, a few enlisted in filibustering expeditions to Mexico. Of the thousands who remained, many carried on businesses founded during the rush. Somehow, through depressions, natural disasters, and five wars, more than a hundred fifty of these firms have stood steadfast to the present day. Their roster is a profile of the forty-niners' needs: hardware dealers, restaurants, wineries, food processors, druggists, work-clothing manufacturers, merchandisers, paint manufacturers, and iron foundries. Of these venerable firms, a half-dozen have achieved national renown.

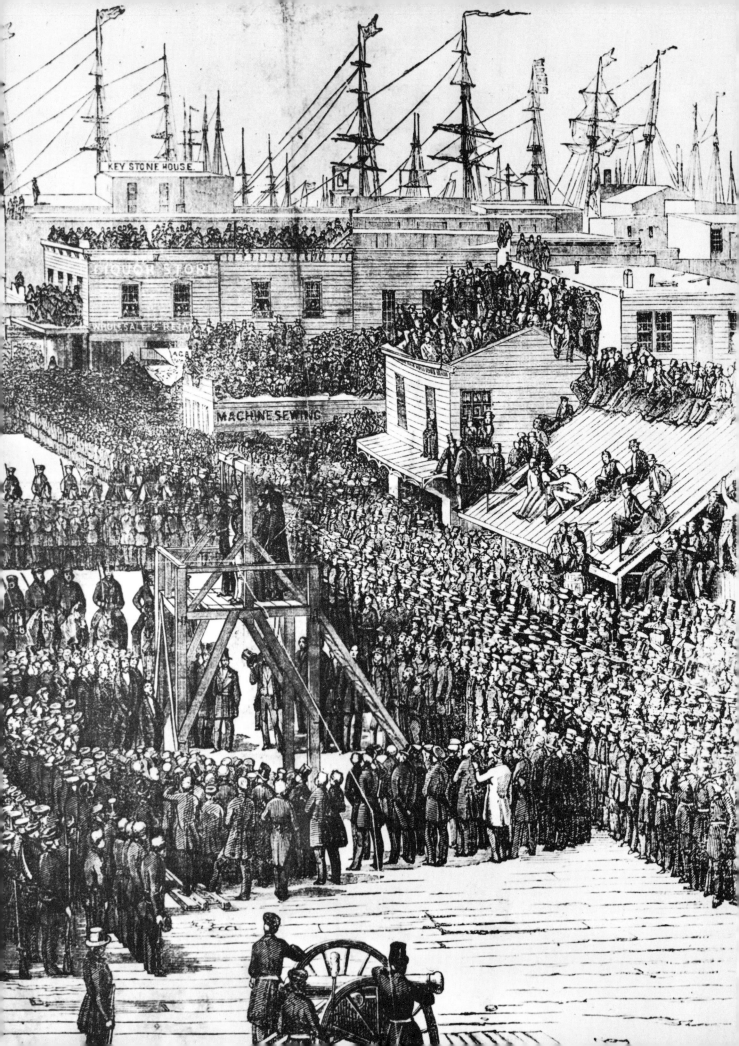

1850-1870

Raw Young State

WITH the Yankee tidal wave that struck the northern part of California came both positive and negative forces that kept the state in an uproar for many tumultuous years.

Pulling the state forward were the familiar Yankee virtues of hard work, ingenuity, and organizational drive, coupled with ingrained traditions of democratic self-government and a faith in the mighty dollar. Newcomers of this red-white-and-blue stripe built up the towns and cities, stocked them with merchandise, culture, and good works, organized transportation, and kept the rapidly growing state from disintegrating of its own momentum.

At the worst, the pioneer virtues permitted exploitation of California's resources under the mandate of individual enterprise. Lacking restraints, entrepreneurs were free to strip forests, wash mountains out to sea, and build cheap resorts in areas of great scenic grandeur.

For several years after the end of the war with Mexico, California lived in a political limbo. Admission to the Union was delayed by Congress from one session to another because of slavery issues. Neither recognized as a territory nor a protectorate, the new acquisition had no government beyond what the military could improvise.

Vigilantes took over law enforcement in the early years of the new state after the failure of constituted authority to control crime. Hangings by the Vigilance Committees of San Francisco, such as the dispatch of Hetherington and Brace, who were hanged for murder (1856), were public spectacles attended by thousands of approving spectators.

A succession of seven military governors kept order for three and a half years, under extralegal authority from Washington. These men had their hands full; as a contemporary noted, "the laws were most variant and variously conceived, the civil law, the Pike County code, the New York code, the common law, maritime law, the law of the plain, military law, and the miners' law, were all jumbled up together, and the Courts were as unique as the government and the laws; they were American-Mexican, military-civil, with a good degree of vigilante."

Despairing of congressional action after Congress had adjourned for the second time without admitting California to the Union, the military governor convened a legislature to draft a state constitution in 1849. Delegates were chosen from ten geographical districts, apportioned according to population. The composition of the group reveals how fully the north dominated the political scenery: twenty-seven from Northern California and only ten from the south.

The convention, which met in Monterey, was a cross-section of the business and political leadership of the day. It included several men who had been active in the affairs of Mexican California, some who had fought against American troops. The group took its mission seriously, worked amicably and democratically. Their most far-reaching decision was to make California a free state, an item they agreed upon unanimously with hardly any debate. The decision would upset the balance of power between free and slave states in the Union, but the convention went on about its ordinary business as if nothing unusual had happened.

After six weeks' deliberation, the delegates signed the document and celebrated with a grand ball and a community festival. The constitution endured for thirty years until it was replaced by the cumbersome document that now governs the state.

Even after admission to the Union, the raw young state was plagued by problems of law enforcement. Lack of responsibility during the rudderless years, a frontier cynicism toward constituted authority, and the prevalence of a lawless element made for a volatile mixture that kept the state simmering.

In the northern cities and mining towns, saloons, gambling parlors, and brothels flourished in the predominantly male society and corrupted local authorities. The southern part of the state felt some of the backwash when northern authorities occasionally applied the heat, but the southland had its own criminal aristocracy. As early as 1842, an English visitor reported that Los Angeles "is the noted abode of the lowest drunkards and gamblers in the country." A sorry mixture of bandits, displaced Indians, and renegades from Mexico gave the pueblo an evil reputation that lasted until the 1870's. By contrast, the countryside dreamed on, still comfortably living out the rancho period, basking in unparalleled prosperity because of northern demands for butter, beef, and wool. When this market dropped away in the sixties because of drought and falling demand, the idle hands on the ranchos gravitated to Los Angeles and added to the witches' brew.

In the absence of adequate constituted authority, the enforcement of law and order was taken over by citizen groups. Working with sobering efficiency, vigilantes meted swift justice. In San Francisco, they set up a formal court, followed prescribed judicial proceedings, and made arrests with their own police. Of ninety-one evil-doers arrested by the Vigilance Committee of 1851, four were hanged, twenty-eight banished, and the remainder released. Hundreds of miscreants got the message and vanished from view. Its work done, the committee dissolved—only to reassemble in strength five years later when the criminals resurfaced.

The reconvening of the committee, caused by the slaying of a crusading editor, brought forth a massive show of strength. This time, eight thousand men responded to the call, well armed with thousands of muskets and thirty cannon. They pre-empted police and judicial authority for several months before they disbanded for good. Although they cleansed the city of corruption, making it for years "the best-governed city in the United States," according to one authority, the committee was criticized for giving public sanction to mob rule and establishing an ugly precedent for paramilitary organizations to operate outside the law.

Unfortunately, one of the disturbing aspects of the pell-mell growth of these early years was the emergence of an intolerant attitude toward dark-skinned minorities by the onrushing Americans, who brought with them bitter memories of conflict with Indians and Mexicans in other parts of the country.

First to feel the Yankee's contempt were the California Indians who were unlucky enough to live in the gold country and the northern river valleys. The newcomers killed or drove out the natives in their paths and took over their tribal lands for mining or farming. Indian population, which had stood at 100,000 in 1852, dropped to 53,000 within three years, and continued to recede until about 1870, when it began a slow recovery, eventually leveling off around 1900.

Under the impact of the American contact, many of the Indians vanished into the hills, some were permitted to remain in their villages, some were settled on reservations, and a hotheaded few turned on their conquerors, burning crops, stealing horses, raiding settlements, and murdering lone prospectors. Some took to banditry.

Indian depredations became so serious that Governor Burnett could tell the legislature in 1851 that "this is a war of extermination that will continue until the Indian race shall become extinct. It is beyond the power or wisdom of man to avert the inevitable destiny." Troops were called in, forts established, and punitive campaigns conducted. The Indians made their last stand in 1872, when a determined handful of warriors held off U.S. troops for several months.

Dark-skinned Latins were next to feel the bite of Yankee prejudice. Exclusion acts passed in the 1850's placed discriminatory taxes on them. Some paid, some gave up their lands and mining claims, thousands returned to Mexico.

In time, even the native-born Californios began

to feel the weight of oppression. Immediately after the conquest, the Spanish-Mexican citizens of the new state had responded agreeably to the American occupation. In Southern California, they comprised a substantial majority of the population for several decades and their leaders were respected by the Americanos. The wealthier rancheros operated large cattle ranches in the hinterland and their titles to the huge grants were regarded as sacrosanct under the terms of the peace treaty.

As the pace of Americanization accelerated, however, the native Californians began to lose out to the aggressive newcomers. A major blow came with the congressional decision to review all Mexican land claims and titles. A special tribunal to hear land cases was set up in 1852. It was expected to last three years but required five to process the mass of litigation. During this time, the court reviewed eight hundred cases, ruled favorably on five hundred, and quashed two hundred. Proof of title was placed on the owner of the land, an expensive, time-consuming action that enlisted battalions of lawyers. Owners had to prove that they had actually received and used the land—a simple human fact that was surprisingly hard to document. The original grants had been casually defined with the most haphazard boundaries, and written records were either nonexistent or too vague to stand up in court.

The full bite of land litigation hit hardest in the north, where the presence of ample water made the land valuable for farming or dairying. Grants were occupied by squatters, farmers with standing crops, and herdsmen with grazing flocks. Trespassers with the temerity to dispute the claims of the original owners often won out in court because of the hopelessly inadequate proof that many grantees brought to the courtroom.

As an example, the Peralta family, among the first to settle in the East Bay, lost their vast holdings to a variety of squatters that occupied their land while it was still being tested in court. By the time the grant was finally certified by the court, two cities, harbor improvements, schools, and a university had been developed on the land, and the Peraltas were permitted to retain only a fragment of their once-great preserve.

The Californios gradually became adjusted to the alien new society that had engulfed them. Many

THE GREAT SEAL OF CALIFORNIA

The Great Seal, introduced in 1849 at the behest of the constitutional convention, features Minerva, the goddess who sprang full grown from the brain of Jupiter, symbolic of California's political birth. Her bear companion, included to gratify the Bear Flaggers, has over the years been shown asleep, chasing its tail, standing up, lying down, and eating hay, grapes, pears, apples, and grain.

Restless Bear: Standing, 1937 (above)

Eating, circa 1920

Dozing, circa 1909

Ruminating, 1849

who felt uncomfortable with the Americanos' restless ways retreated into their own community. Many adapted to their new country and distinguished themselves in community and state affairs.

All in all, the rambunctious Americanization of California in the first years of statehood produced an unstable but vital society that somehow carried the state through its growing pains.

Vigilante Law and Order

Ruffians from all over the world trooped to California to fleece the Argonauts of their gold. Although they infested the whole of the gold country, they found their warmest sanctuary in the gateway cities, San Francisco, Sacramento, and Stockton, where they were able to carry on their misdeeds with little interference from harassed or venal authorities.

The best-publicized outpouring of organized indignation occurred in San Francisco in 1851 and again in 1856, when the famous vigilance committees purged the city of evil-doers. Similar organizations appeared in Los Angeles, San Diego, and Santa Barbara. In Los Angeles, however, the vigilantes turned criminals over to the regular courts for trial and sentencing instead of punishing them themselves.

Five disastrous fires consumed the heart of wooden San Francisco between 1849 and 1851. Mostly the work of hoodlums who looted business establishments in the confusion, fires brought about formation of the first Vigilance Committee.

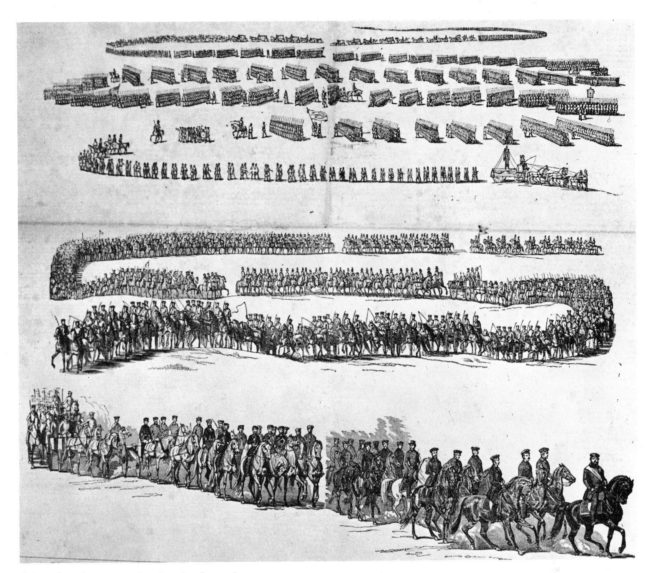

A massive demonstration by the Second Vigilance Committee in August 1856 revealed the armed might of the paramilitary organization. Presence of such a force outside the law disturbed state and city officials, prompted creation of an opposition group, the Law and Order Party, which nearly warred with the vigilantes.

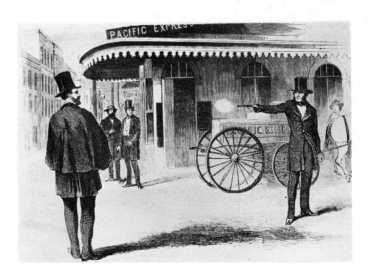

Reactivation of the Vigilance Committee in 1856, after it had been dormant for four years, was caused by the shooting of crusading editor James King of William by a racketeer, James P. Casey.

Eclipse of the Indian

A tragic casualty of the decades following the Gold Rush was the California Indian, who was overrun, slaughtered, and driven from his ancestral home in Northern California by the avalanche of Yankees who brought with them bitter memories of Indian treachery in other parts of the country. The newcomers were quick with the trigger and were members of the good-Indian/dead-Indian school.

Retaliatory raids by Indian braves in the Klamath region and in other northern localities provoked fearful retribution. The Indians made a final stand in the Modoc Lava Beds, but were defeated after a costly siege. The federal government established army posts to protect settlers from Indian depredations and opened reservations to accommodate the splintered tribes. Finally, after two decades of conflict, the natives resigned themselves to adopting enough of the Yankee's ways to survive. Some of the tribes even managed to preserve some of their rich heritage and to contribute to the cultural and commercial enrichment of the state.

Skirmishes between Indians and settlers began as soon as the pioneers pushed into Indian lands, as depicted in this heroic scene of Frémont leading a charge against six hundred Indian bowmen at Reddings Rancho in 1846. Hearing of an Indian plot to burn settlers' crops, Frémont "at a single stroke, in one day, utterly annihilated the Indian combination and rescued the settlers from threatening ruin, without loss of a man."

The last battle of consequence, the Modoc War of 1872–73, resulted in the murder of General E. R. S. Canby and members of a truce team by the renegade Indian leader Captain Jack. Up to that time General Canby was the only United States general to have been killed in action.

A determined band of 150 warriors held off 1200 troops for six months in one of the costliest Indian wars in the nation's history. Success of the Modocs encouraged other tribes later to resist the white man in Yellowstone and on the Great Plains. The battle attracted wide attention and drew correspondents from New York and Europe. Harper's Weekly (right), which featured it for several months, depicted the battling Indians as degenerates.

Bandits Around Every Bend

Throughout the 1850's, gangs of bandits roamed the countryside, pillaging, murdering, and fighting running gun battles with ranchers, posses, vigilantes, and rangers specially deputized to hunt them down.

The scourge of brigandage was partly a reaction against discrimination directed at the dark-skinned minority in the gold region. Oppressive legislation, including the onerous "Greaser Law," of 1855 (the epithet was actually in the text of the law), plus a tax on foreigners of twenty dollars a month, stirred antigringo sentiments among the Latins. In 1850, vigilantes drove ten thousand Sonorans out of the southern mines, forcing them to take the long trail back to northern Mexico.

Resentment of Anglo domination was widespread and deep-seated. The young bucks who chose to become outlaws had the tacit or actual support of much of the Spanish-Mexican community.

The wild-eyed bandit Joaquín Murietta was everywhere at once, robbing the rich to feed the poor. Archetype of the marauders of the 1850's, Joaquín terrorized Mariposa County for two years before he was captured and beheaded by state rangers. The exploits of this folk hero were known throughout Latin America and Spain. One biography published in South America had him going to Washington to plead, somewhat anachronistically, with President Thomas Jefferson.

Joaquín's head, preserved in a jar of aguardiente, was a gruesome attraction in saloons—occasionally in more than one at the same time.

In later years, banditry lost its Robin Hood aura and settled down to the lucrative specialty of stage robbery, which continued until the railroads took over the expressing of treasure. In a fourteen-year period (1770–84), Wells Fargo stages were relieved of nearly $400,000 in 313 holdups. In the rare photograph above, a masked highwayman poses nervously for the cameraman while robbing the Yosemite stage.

A simple, stark room on the second floor of Colton Hall in Monterey was the setting for the constitutional convention of 1849, which ended with a dramatic community celebration. As described by the correspondent for the New York Tribune, "the delegates affixed their names to the completed Constitution, and at this moment a signal was given; the American colors ran up the flagstaff in front of the Government buildings, and streamed out on the air. A second afterward the first gun boomed from the fort, and its stirring echoes came back from one hill after another, till they were lost in the distance . . . As the signing went on, gun followed gun from the fort, the echoes reverberating grandly around the bay, till finally, as the loud ring of the thirty-first was heard, there was a shout: 'That's for California!'"

Capitol No. 1—at Monterey (1849)

Capitol No. 2—at San Jose (1849–51)

Capitol No. 3—at Vallejo (1851–53)

Capitol No. 4—at Benicia (1853–54)

Capital on Wheels

The new state government was launched in political chaos. Unrecognized by Congress even as a territory, the state limped along on quasi-official authority. A constitution was drafted in 1849 and ratified by the citizens of the nonstate, and a jury-rigged government was established with neither congressional precedent nor approval.

Once sanctioned by Congress, the legislature got down to work. Early on the agenda was the question of a place to meet. Within a period of four years, the lawmakers skipped around among five capitals before finally settling in Sacramento. Many legislators regretted leaving Monterey with its wooded setting and crisp climate for the boiler-room weather of Sacramento, but the river town lay closer to the heart of the emerging state than the original capital. Monterey dwindled in importance, settling into a leisurely Spanish-Mexican town.

Capitol No. 5—at Sacramento (1854)—was the final stopping place of the wandering legislature. While in San Jose, the lawmakers earned the dubious title of "The Legislature of a Thousand Drinks." General Vallejo lured the body with the prospect of 156 acres and $370,000 worth of new buildings, but when he was unable to deliver, the lawmakers moved to the Benicia City Hall and, finally, accompanied by barbers and bartenders, steamed up-river to Sacramento.

Tale of Two Cities

Ever since Gold Rush days, San Franciscans have enjoyed looking down their noses at Los Angeles. But up to 1848 there was little to distinguish either settlement, and both were outclassed by Monterey, the provincial capital.

The Gold Rush metamorphosed San Francisco into a metropolis but left Los Angeles almost untouched. By 1850, San Francisco had 35,000 residents, Los Angeles only 1600 —half as many as Grass Valley. In the general election of 1852, San Francisco led the balloting with 8000 votes, Los Angeles polled 300—38 less than the town of Volcano. As late as 1865, Los Angeles was off the main mail routes, had only one newspaper and no banks. Railroads considered the town so unpromising that they demanded a heavy subsidy before entering.

The imbalance lasted until the 1880's, when a stampede of immigrants poured into Southern California and altered Los Angeles as dramatically as the first great rush had changed San Francisco.

San Francisco (above) in 1850 had already begun to take shape as a metropolis and soon could boast of cultural amenities, commercial enterprises, and sophisticated vices unduplicated west of the Alleghenys. The Gold Rush impelled it half a century out in front of all other California cities. Los Angeles (below) in 1857 was the trading center for a widespread cattle industry based on the Mexican ranchos. Tar-roofed adobes were scattered along meandering unpaved streets. In essence a Mexican frontier pueblo, it was dominated by Spanish-speaking Californios for several decades. Out of 2500 residents in 1852, there were only seventy-five Yankees. Many of the Americans who settled there in the next few years were outcasts from the north who helped to stir up trouble.

POPULATION COMPARISON		
	San Francisco	Los Angeles
1846	50	650
1850	34,776	1,610
1860	56,802	4,385
1870	149,473	5,728
1880	233,959	11,183
1890	298,997	50,395
1900	342,782	102,479
1910	416,912	319,198
1920	506,676	576,673

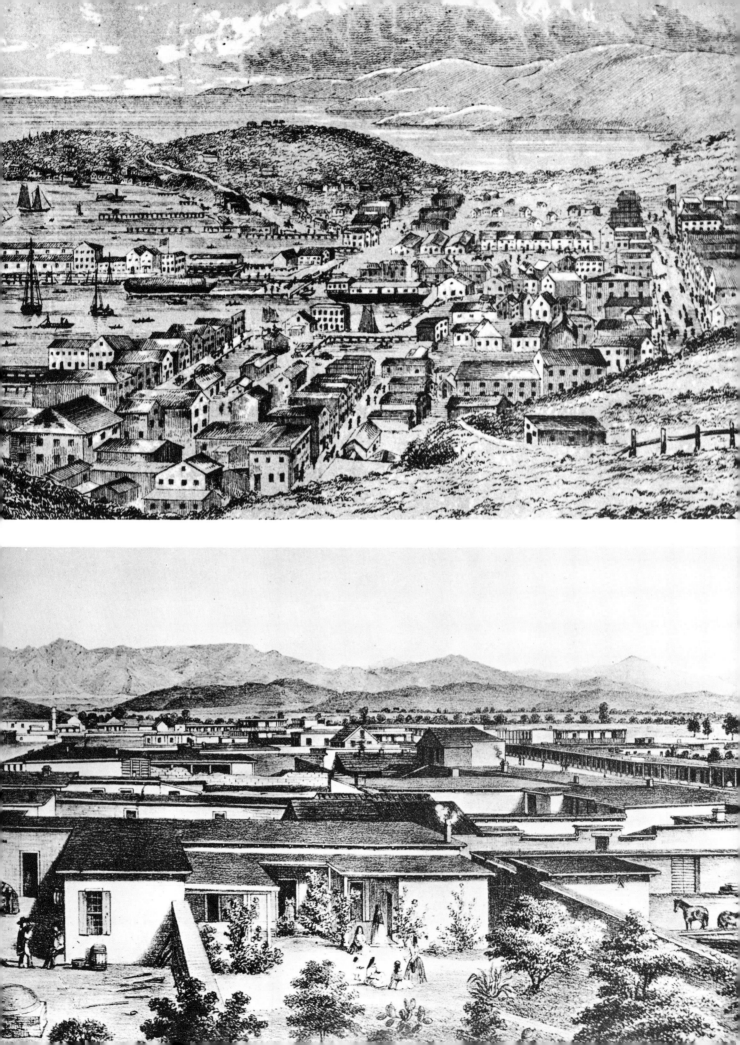

Giant coast redwood trees make up a trainload apiece. Short-line railroads hauled the huge logs to mills in the woods and then carried the lumber to doghole ports along the rugged coast, where it was shot down chutes to lumber schooners daringly anchored offshore.

Trees Become Cities

Of all the natural resources waiting in California to be converted to man's use, none was more desperately needed than timber to build the burgeoning cities. And of all the trees selected for the ax, none proved more valuable than the unique and stately redwoods. This remarkable wood had been appreciated earlier by the Indians, Spaniards, and Russians for its unusual properties. It did not shrink or rot, was unaffected by the weather, and was light and easy to dress. Starting in the 1850's, loggers stripped thousands of acres of the trees, eventually alarming conservationists who launched a campaign to save some of the groves before they were all gone. The race between loggers and tree savers resulted in preserving thousands of acres for posterity, sometimes with the active help of the more farsighted lumbermen themselves.

Too good for its own good, redwood has so many unique properties that its commercial exploitation was unavoidable. An early booklet listed dozens of uses: caskets, cigar boxes, water pipes, lead pencils, camera stock, organ pipes.

Down goes a Big Tree in the Sierra, leaving "a lonesome place against the sky." Even these three-thousand-year-old trees were not immune to the ax. Logs rocketed down flumes sixty-five miles to mills in the San Joaquin Valley.

"Hoofed locusts" was John Muir's contemptuous term for the tens of thousands of sheep that clipped off the ground cover on the Sierra watersheds, causing spring floods and summer droughts in the valleys below.

Naturalist John Muir came to Yosemite in 1869 at the age of thirty, adopted the Sierra as his own, and fought to save it from abuse. He helped found the Sierra Club (1892); served as its president twenty-two years.

Protection for Natural Wonders and Curiosities

Because of their inaccessibility, California's renowned scenic wonders did not reveal themselves until the 1850's, but, once discovered, they soon became objects of exploitation. Resorts began to appear in Yosemite. Some of the majestic Sierra Big Trees were felled and shipped East for display as museum curiosities, and their enormous stumps were converted into tourist attractions. As the mountain trails became known, stockmen crowded thousands of cattle and sheep onto the high meadows, creating a serious erosion threat from overgrazing. Expelled time and again from the high country, the wily stockmen persisted in trespassing for decades.

Concerned citizens foresaw a need to protect the wilderness and launched a crusade for legislative controls. With the help of the powerful Southern Pacific political machine, they successfully hammered through a sequence of bellwether laws that protected most of the scenic wonders from commercialization and set the stage for later development of the national park system for the country as a whole. Yosemite Valley and Mariposa Grove were made a state park in 1864—first in the nation—and twenty-six years later were designated a national park, along with Sequoia and General Grant Grove.

Cavalry patrols were a common sight in Yosemite and Sequoia for twenty-four years after the two parks were established. The frugal Congress that created the parks (1890) neglected to appropriate funds for administration, and the Department of Interior had to contract with the Army for needed manpower.

Typical of commercial misuse of the Big Trees, the stump of the original Discovery Tree serves as a dance floor for a Fourth of July cotillion in 1854. Discovered in 1852, the tree became a tourist attraction and was felled (five men, twenty-two days) so tourists could buy bits of souvenir bark. The stump was later enclosed with a pavilion, the fallen trunk made into a bowling alley.

1857–1869

End of Insularity

ALTHOUGH California had mushroomed in a decade into a self-contained economy, the booming state was stalled in its growth by physical remoteness from the economic life streams of the nation.

Between the coast and the Mississippi Valley, then the leading edge of the developing nation, lay two formidable mountain ranges, a swath of trackless desert, and a thousand miles of open plain. No major east-west rivers breeched this physical barrier, and people and freight still had to rely on modes of overland and ocean transportation little changed from pre-Gold Rush days.

Mail service was exasperatingly slow. Thanks to a monopoly by a steamship company, it took two to three weeks for the fastest mail to arrive from New York or the Mississippi Valley. Los Angeles sometimes had to wait seven or eight months for mail delivery from the East. In 1855, the town of San Luis Obispo had received only eight deliveries in eighteen months.

If far-off California were to escape stagnation, it had to establish more rapid and reliable means of communicating and exchanging goods with the rest of the country. Rapid mail service by pony carrier (1860) and overland stage (1857) halved the time for delivery of dispatches from New York, but neither service could handle more than a small

fraction of the mail. Even camels were tried out in the desert routes.

The notion of flying people and mail through the air was advanced by ardent balloonists in the sixties, and crackpot inventors proposed one contraption after another for rocket service. Carrier pigeons flew onionskin messages to coastal islands and remote mountain settlements.

The clear answer to California's strangling isolation was coast-to-coast rail service. The story of the state's release from insularity is basically the story of the coming of the transcontinental train.

Proposals for such a route had been advanced in Washington in the 1840's—while California was still a Mexican province. Soon after the state was admitted, a series of surveys was conducted by the War Department to determine the most feasible east-west routes and their feeder lines. Teams of topographical engineers reconnoitered the land west of the Mississippi and in 1855 recommended four practical routes in a monumental report that is still consulted as a major source on the geology, botany, ethnology, and history of the trans-Mississippi west. Within California, the engineers surveyed possible north-south routes, as well as trans-Sierra passages, and their recommendations later formed the basis for the rapid development of intrastate lines in the 1870's.

Unfortunately, the proposals for the Pacific Railroad became embroiled in sectional politics. Proponents for each of the transcontinental routes entrenched themselves and forced a stalemate. Even within California, partisans of Los Angeles, San Diego, and San Francisco, seeking the terminus for

Decorated and polished, festooned with celebrants, locomotives of the Central and Union Pacific railroads stand nose to nose at Promontory Point, Utah, May 10, 1869, in honor of the linking of California to the rest of the nation by rail.

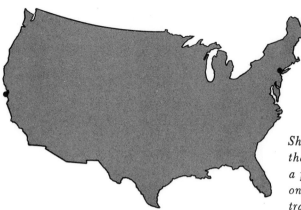
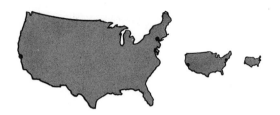

Shrinking continent: To a traveler setting out for California from the East Coast in the early 1800's, the intervening land mass was a formidable obstacle. It took from 6 to 9 months to pass from one coast to another by ship or on foot. Later, conestogas, pack trains, fast stagecoaches, and finally the railroad successively shrank the continent to a mass that could be traversed in 10 days.

their respective cities, fought each other instead of uniting behind a drive to bring rails to the state.

The impasse was dissolved by the outbreak of the Civil War, which eliminated the southern routes. Construction of the railroad was authorized by Congress in 1862 as a military necessity and as a means for holding California in the Union. The news of the passage of the bill was received in San Francisco with jubilation. A "long and brilliant procession marched in a blaze of lights, while the air was thick with smoke and loud with the music of clamoring bands, shriekings of the steam whistle, and the thunders of cannon."

The bill actually authorized the construction of two distinct roads and designated by name the companies that were to carry out the task. The Union Pacific was to lay track from Omaha to the western boundary of Nevada, and "there to meet and connect with the line of the Central Pacific of California."

The California company was the brain child of a brilliant young civil engineer named Theodore D. Judah, who had become excited by the vision of building a transcontinental line over the Sierra. On his own initiative, he made more than twenty trips across the mountains, some in the dead of winter, seeking a practical route. When he was sure that he had found it, he sought financial backing for a coast-to-coast line.

By dangling the bait of substantial government subsidies and prospects for monopolizing the lucrative freight moving in and out of the silver-mining district of Nevada, he enlisted a quartet of Sacramento businessmen—two dry-goods merchants and

two hardware dealers—and together they formed the Central Pacific in 1861.

A short time later, Judah began to have misgivings about his associates, and he left for New York to find new backers. Tragically, he died of yellow fever while crossing the Isthmus, thus leaving the fruits of his imagination, energy, and zeal in the hands of the Sacramentans.

At the outset, the "Big Four" were neither very widely known nor very wealthy, but within a few years they became the most powerful railroad group in the West, and for three decades were a controlling factor in the state's economy. Stanford, Crocker, Huntington, and Hopkins were strong-willed and stubborn as individuals, but as a team they performed as a well-nigh-unbeatable unit. Their secret was a division of responsibility that they adhered to until death dissolved the combine.

The task before them would have unhinged lesser men. Their first problem was to acquire an ocean of capital to finance the costly construction over the Sierra. They sought it wherever they could lay their hands on it, principally public resources, from Washington down to the smallest hamlet in the path of the juggernaut. They assembled a conglomeration of subsidies, loans, bonds, and outright gifts from federal, state, county, and city governments. The most princely allotments came from Congress, which awarded the Central Pacific for each mile of construction 12,800 acres of public land and a cash bonus of $18,000 that soared to $48,000 for mountain construction.

With ample money in hand—more than ample, as it later turned out—the Central Pacific still had to overcome the most formidable construction obstacles. Every spike, rail, locomotive, and hand tool had to be purchased in the East, shipped to San Francisco via the Isthmus, and hauled to the railroad. Because of the Civil War, purchasing agents had to compete against the military for steel, railroad equipment, and cargo space. In addition, they had to outwit the Union Pacific agents who were bidding for the same supplies.

A special incentive for rapid track laying was a change in the law in 1864 that permitted the Central Pacific to build eastward beyond the California border into the domain originally reserved for the rival line. Crocker hoped that his invincible Chinese could beat the Union Pacific's Irish track-layers into Salt Lake City, and his crews raced all the way across Nevada and were deep into Utah before they were stopped by the advancing rails of the other road at Promontory. It was here that the rails were joined in a historic ceremony in 1869.

Once the line was in operation, the rail magnates found themselves in a position of regal power within California. By withholding or granting economic concessions, they could determine the fate of towns, cities, and agricultural regions. Inevitably, such a concentration of power led to abuses and corruption and engendered an aura of public ill-will that lasted for two generations. Unfortunately, the high-handed exercise of its public trust by the rail monopoly obscured the fact that the railroad did contribute mightily to the state's development and helped prepare the way for industrial pre-eminence.

Along with the development of rail transportation, a corresponding acceleration of oceanic service made a further breach in California's isolation and marked the beginning of commercial interdependence with the countries around the Pacific rim.

American trading vessels had visited Spanish California in the early 1800's, on their way to the Orient. The vessels carried furs picked up along the West Coast, many of them from the mission padres, and exchanged them for oriental luxuries. After the Gold Rush, clippers began to cut a path across the Pacific, carrying the burgeoning production of California's fields and farms. With the appearance of ocean-going steamships in the 1850's, regularly scheduled runs were begun. The Pacific Mail Steamship Company received a charter to carry mail to the Orient in 1857, and soon there

were several lines competing for passengers and freight from the Orient and the Hawaiian Islands.

The primitive port facilities in Southern California began to show signs of development. San Pedro became involved in a protracted struggle with the railroads over harbor improvements. A custom-house was authorized for the port in 1858, and foreign goods could thenceforth be unloaded there without having to be transshipped with onerous fees from San Francisco. Harbor improvements were planned for San Diego and Santa Barbara, but major development of the southern ports had to await the commercial build-up of the area, which did not occur until late in the nineteenth century.

THE CURSE OF CALIFORNIA

Not everyone appreciated the accomplishments of the Central Pacific's successor, the Southern Pacific. Critics lampooned the railroad for its monopolistic practices for years.

The Longest Stage Ride in the World

Abominable mail connections with the East prompted the creation of the first transcontinental stage line in 1858 to supplement the existing service. In that year, the Postmaster General awarded a contract to John Butterfield to construct and operate a mail stage from San Francisco to St. Louis, following an all-year route through the south. An administrative genius, Butterfield had his Overland Mail running within a year. Stage stations were built every ten miles along the 2700-mile route, much of it through uninhabited or hostile Indian territory. More than a thousand men, 1500 animals, and a hundred Concord coaches were involved in the enterprise. Stages rolled night and day, regardless of weather or Indian uprisings, carrying 170 pounds of mail (at three cents per half ounce) and six numbed passengers from one terminus to the other in twenty-three days. The line operated, with time out for the Civil War, until displaced by railroad competition.

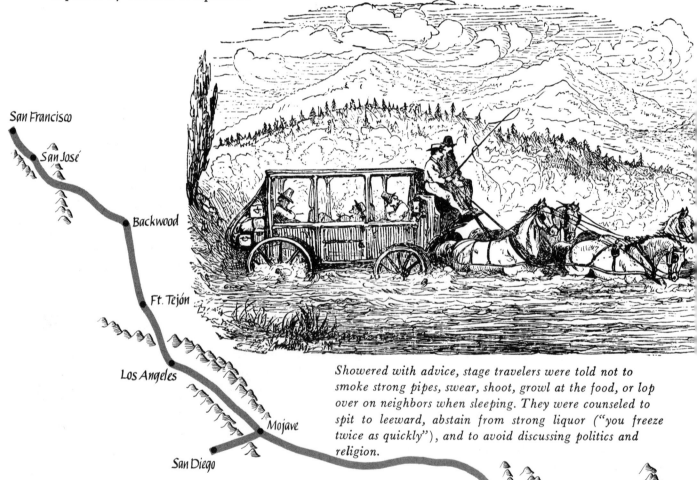

Showered with advice, stage travelers were told not to smoke strong pipes, swear, shoot, growl at the food, or lop over on neighbors when sleeping. They were counseled to spit to leeward, abstain from strong liquor ("you freeze twice as quickly"), and to avoid discussing politics and religion.

San Francisco
San José
Backwood
Ft. Tejón
Los Angeles
Mojave
San Diego
Tucson

The southern path of the Butterfield stage route was free of snow in winter, open when northern lines were blocked.

A terrifying sight for stage travelers, roads over the Sierra were narrow shelves chiseled out of the mountain sides, often with nothing but a thousand feet of fresh air on the downside. Turns were so abrupt that lead horses vanished around the bends. On steep grades, passengers had to help boost the heavy stage up the slope; and on the descent, they hung on in sheer terror while the vehicle rocketed down with smoking brakes.

St. Louis

Little Rock

On a long ride, compacted passengers were shaken into a solid ball of humanity that "rose and fell as a single unit with each lurch of the coach."

Paso

Unnerving to man and beast, camel caravans appeared in the mountains in the 1860's as part of an Army experiment. The fractious animals proved their worth but were considered no match for the honest, hard-working horse and mule.

Experiments in Communication

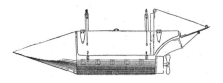

To New York in thirty hours by aluminum airship was the promise of this vehicle.

Two grandiose attempts to solve California's isolation have become enshrined in Western legend. Both plans relied on animals for their fulfillment, and both were done in by a mechanical device.

The first was a scheme to conquer the trackless desert with a camel corps, initiated by the Army in 1857. The beasts proved themselves along the border, and a caravan was dispatched 1200 miles to California to test a supply route to the coast. They arrived in 1862 and frittered away an unhappy decade before the corps was disbanded and the dromedaries auctioned off. Penetration of the railroad into the desert areas, along with other factors, killed off the noble experiment.

Equally bold was the attempt to speed the mails with a two-thousand-mile horse race, performed by the pony express for eighteen months (1860–61). The enterprise was an operational success but a financial disappointment. Unable to compete with the telegraph, it shut down after the wire reached the coast.

Pony express riders were legendary for their derring-do, outracing Indians, floods, prairie fires, and buffalo stampedes in their purposeful gallop. Carefully selected, they were expected to cover a hundred miles in eleven hours; each took an oath that he would not drink, fight, or swear while on duty. Offering a dramatic reduction in time between San Francisco and New York from twenty-three to ten days, the pony express attracted high-priority mail.

Pony expressmen wave to linemen stringing wire that ended the riders' careers. The express was never a money-maker and could not compete with the telegraph.

Heavy snow pack in the Sierra passes—deepest in the country—forced the Central Pacific to evolve techniques for keeping its tracks clear in winter. At the start, special trains rammed a path through the snow with a plow shaped like the prow of a battleship. When the plow could push no more, the battery of engines backed up and took another concerted run at the embankment.

Steel Across the Sierra

Linking California with the East by rail was an engineering and construction feat of the first magnitude.

Chief obstacle was the massive Sierra monolith lying across the path of the railroad. The right of way had to climb seven thousand feet from the Sacramento Valley, blast its way through jumbled granite country, and twist abruptly down four thousand feet to the Carson Sink. Gradients had to be held to an easy incline negotiable by the short-winded locomotives of the day. Although provision had been made for deep snow, the pack proved much heavier than anticipated, delaying construction and stalling trains.

An army of 12,000 Chinese, imported to clear the right of way and lay the track, made an astonishing record. Using only the simplest tools, they worked so efficiently and tirelessly that they put the Central Pacific far ahead of its rival building from the east.

A railroad link with the East was made possible by Chinese laborers, who, with pick and shovel and one-man dump carts, advanced the rails over the most difficult terrain.

Once cleared by the plow, the trench through the snow still called for large gangs of shovelers. Unexpectedly heavy snows forced the railroad to erect forty miles of snowshed across the higher elevations.

The first timetable for the first unit of the first transcontinental line was issued while tracks were still being laid eastward. The Central Pacific was absorbed into the Southern Pacific twenty years later.

Famous Techachapi Loop, where trains make a complete circle in the mountains north of Los Angeles, was an engineering marvel of the day (1876), designed to ease the climb for locomotives ascending the steep barrier. When completed, it opened the first rail connection between Los Angeles and the north.

Small independent short lines, such as the California Western Railroad and Navigation Company, twisted their way in and out of the more remote sections of the state. Best-known survivor of this species is The Skunk, from Fort Bragg to Willits.

Intrastate Rail Lines

Completion of the transcontinental line—"Uncle Sam's Waistband"—started an intrastate railroad construction boom that lasted thirty years, crisscrossed the state with tracks, and opened new areas to farming and commerce.

Even before the wedding of the rails, train whistles had been echoing in the valleys and mountains. Short lines rumbled through the forests hauling logs and mine tailings. Along the north coast, logging lines carried lumber to the bluffs where it was shot down greased chutes to schooners anchored offshore.

Major competition for internal traffic ranged over the state, with the Central Pacific (Southern Pacific after 1884) dominating the no-quarter struggle for future markets. Feeder lines reached Los Angeles in 1876, San Diego in 1885, and Santa Barbara in 1887, giving these cities direct rail connections with the East. Competing interstate lines wedged their way into the state after the Santa Fe opened the path in 1887.

Trestle building became a fine engineering art as rails penetrated the mountainous areas of the state. Even short mining and logging lines had to bridge deep canyons in traversing the precipitous terrain.

Overnight steamers to Sacramento offered luxury transportation that was popular until well into the twentieth century. As this 1877 scene suggests, they were opulently furnished with elaborately turned moldings, red plush upholstery, marble-topped tables, gilt-framed mirrors in the latest Victorian décor. Their passenger lists included a mixed clientele of businessmen, miners, and families.

Ripsnorting River Days

Like a many-fingered extension of San Francisco Bay, the river system of the Central Valley expanded the reach of water transportation to cities a hundred miles inland. From the start of the Gold Rush, the Sacramento River carried a heavy volume of mixed watercraft. By the end of 1850, twenty-eight steamers were operating between Sacramento and San Francisco, and sixty-three deep-water sailing vessels, including a 241-ton square-rigger, had tacked their way up and down the tortuous channel.

Scaled-down versions of Mississippi paddle-wheelers competed mercilessly for business. Some shallow-draft steamers made it all the way to Red Bluff. They drew so little water they "could navigate on dry land after a rain storm." Silting of river channels and cutthroat competition from the railroads greatly reduced river traffic after the 1870's.

Pride of the Sacramento run, the
Chrysopolis, *the "Golden City," was built
in San Francisco in 1862, dominated the
river for more than a decade. Her
down-river run of five hours and
eighteen minutes was never equaled.
After the decline in passenger service,
she was remodeled as a ferryboat and
sailed for forty-five years under the name
Oakland.*

*Reckless river captains, ever willing to
accept a challenge for a race, wreaked
senseless carnage on the river in the
early years of steamboating. Between
1850 and 1864, ten vessels exploded,
killing and maiming hundreds. The
explosion of the* Yosemite, *pictured at
the right, killed forty passengers in 1865.*

Gate to Pacific Shores

Key port for the West Coast after the Gold Rush, the bustling port of San Francisco early got a hammer lock on the commerce of the Pacific. In 1857, a contract to carry mail to Japan and China was awarded to the Pacific Mail Steamship Company, which assigned giant wooden side-wheelers to the thirty-two-day run to Hong Kong.

An expanding trade with the Hawaiian Islands and the Orient compensated the steamship companies for the loss of traffic caused by the opening of the transcontinental railroad in 1869. No longer was the steamer the only means for carrying bulk freight from the East Coast, and steamship owners had to look for new worlds. The trade with the western Pacific grew, attracting competing American and foreign lines. By 1890, San Francisco had become the third most important port in the world, surpassed in ship movements only by Liverpool and the coal port of Newcastle.

A large quantity of whalebone drying in the yard of a whaling company reveals why San Francisco was called the "New Bedford of the Pacific" in the 1880's. The whaling fleet ranged over the North Pacific in summer, wintered in Oakland. Whale oil was shipped east over the transcontinental railroad beginning in the 1870's.

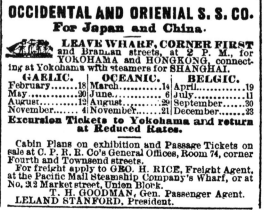
Cargo in great variety moved through the busy port. Docked at Broadway Pier are down-Easters on the left and British lime-juicers on the right. Ships carried grain, lumber, kerosene, machinery, and even ice to Pacific ports, and brought back rice, sugar, silk, tea, hemp, coal, and tallow. Some carried passengers (left) on scheduled runs.

Luxurious coastwise steamers, such as the Orizaba, *plied between California ports from 1865 on, carrying mail, freight, and thousands of passengers a year. Some of the Panama–San Francisco ships likewise visited southern ports.*

Enormous log rafts, assembled in the Pacific Northwest, were towed all the way to San Diego, where they were broken up and milled into lumber.

Late-blooming Ports

Port facilities in Southern California developed slowly, partly because of San Francisco's entrenched monopoly of maritime commerce and partly because the area lacked an adequate industrial base to support a major harbor.

San Diego, San Pedro, and Wilmington participated in a flourishing coastwise traffic. Ships sailing between Panama and San Francisco stopped there regularly. Lumber schooners from the Mendocino coast rendezvoused at San Pedro, but on the whole, extensive trade with the ports of the world still had to wait.

The great landlocked bay of San Diego offered the greatest potential for a world port, but the commercial growth in that corner of the state lagged so far behind that of Los Angeles that it was the unpromising mud flats off San Pedro that ultimately received the appropriations and the capital improvements when the southern ports began to move ahead in the seventies.

*The dumping of thousands of tons of rock to form a breakwater off Wilmington
in 1892 marked the tardy beginning of major port development for Los Angeles.
At the time, two competing ports at San Pedro and Wilmington provided meager
harbor facilities for the Los Angeles area, but after the turn of the century, adroit
gerrymandering extended the Los Angeles city limits to tidewater and gobbled up
both ports within a newly created Los Angeles Harbor.*

Boomland

NORTHERN California had its Gold Rush. Southern California had its Great Boom. Spaced forty years apart, these two seismic happenings changed the character of the state.

Where the lure of picking up fortunes in gold had drawn thousands of men to California in 1849, it was the prospect of amassing fortunes in real estate that attracted a second wave of immigrants in the 1880's. Thousands of families, speculators, and "Escrow Indians" jammed the transcontinental trains destined for Los Angeles, and for an unbridled eighteen months, they carved up the landscape of Southern California into city lots, which they sold and resold in a grand speculative debauch. Miraculously, many of the boom towns took root, and though scores vanished into thin air and hundreds of speculators lost fortunes in paper profits, the net effect of the extravaganza was progressive, and the southern half of the state caught up with the north in economic and political maturity.

The Great Boom did not happen overnight. Although it was precipitated by the railroads, the stage had already been set by a decade of increasing agricultural prosperity, brought about by a number of factors.

By 1880, many of the vast Mexican ranchos, broken up in the collapse of the cattle industry in the 1860's, had been parceled out into farms or

A dapper assembly of orange pickers and growers strikes a whimsical pose for a photographer in 1880. The golden fruit attracted waves of immigrants —drawing some with a foretaste of tropical paradise and others with a vision of economic gain.

residential tracts, and their shaky land titles settled in the courts. In addition, thousands of acres of good farmland had been put on the market by the railroads at relatively low prices, and as the rails crisscrossed the state they opened a path from the farm to the market for wheat, oranges, grapes, wine, cotton, tea, silk, tobacco, and coffee. Developments in irrigation opened vast tracts of wasteland to flourishing production of fruits and field crops. Scientific principles worked out in the state's unique agricultural colleges introduced advanced techniques in erosion control, planting, irrigation, harvesting, and processing. Implausible machines chugged their way through the fields, furrowing, weeding, and picking.

So great was the production, and the local pride in its quality, that a Hall of Produce was opened in Los Angeles to display the abundance of the county's fields and groves.

Word of the growing prosperity in agriculture filtered out of the state. Letters, magazine articles, and books stirred interest in California's climate, agricultural opportunities, and subtropical atmosphere. A steady flow of the curious and the convinced entrained for Southern California from all parts of the country. The well-to-do came out in Mr. George M. Pullman's commodious sleeping, drawing-room, and hotel cars. The less well-to-do crawled along in emigrant cars, likened to "a flat-roofed Noah's ark" by Robert Louis Stevenson, who rode to California in one.

The promotional chorus began to swell in volume and stridency, thanks largely to the aggressiveness of the railroads, which had vast acreages of land to sell and trains to keep filled with passengers and freight. The roads were a major voice in a loose combination of steamship companies, trade associations, state societies, chambers of commerce, and colonizing groups that engaged in a campaign to induce the rest of the world to come to California. By the climax of the campaign (1889–90), it is doubtful if there was a man, woman, or child in the country who had not seen a picture of a redwood tree or Yosemite Falls or tasted a California orange. The loudest call came from Southern California, which had the most to gain from an influx of tourists, settlers, and visitors. As early as 1885, a Northern California newspaper could wryly comment that "the average Eastern mind conceives of California as a small tract of country in and about Los Angeles."

Of the many books written about California in the 1870's probably none had more influence than Charles Nordhoff's *California: for Health, Pleasure, and Residence,* published in 1872. Partially subsidized by the Central Pacific, Nordhoff minimized the discomforts and inconveniences of living in California or passing through as a traveler, but his report was more believable than most of the flamboyant travel literature of the day, and persuaded many of his readers to come West.

To reassure timid or hypercritical Easterners, he wrote: "There are no dangers to travelers on the beaten track in California; there are no inconveniences which a child or a tenderly reared woman would not laugh at; . . . and when you have spent a half dozen weeks in the State, you will perhaps return with a notion that New York is the true frontier land, and that you have nowhere in the United States seen so complete a civilization."

This, he explained, was due to the quality of the Californians themselves. "When gold was discovered," he noted, "wherever an Eastern family had three or four boys, the ablest, most energetic one, came hither. Of that great multitude of picked men, again, the weakly broke down under the strain; they died of disease or bad whisky, or they returned home. The remainder you see here, and you ought not to wonder that they are above your Eastern average in intelligence, energy, and thrift."

As to the virtues of traveling in California, he flatly declared "in no part of the continent is pleasure-traveling so exquisite and unalloyed a pleasure as in California. The country inns are clean, the beds good, the food abundant and almost always well cooked, and the charges moderate; and the journey by rail from New York to San Francisco is in itself delightful as well as instructive."

For reasons hard to comprehend today, part of the promotional campaign was directed to invalids, specifically consumptives. Nordhoff included in his book a chapter for the ailing and a special appendix for consumptives. Prestigious hotels such as the Coronado, Del Monte, Raymond, and Arlington all advertised their facilities for invalids, such as mud baths, mineral water, "special treatments." Real estate broadsides often made a direct appeal to health seekers. A magazine advertisement in 1887 for Oneonta by the Sea—a short-lived plat on San Diego Bay—stressed the usual advantages of scen-

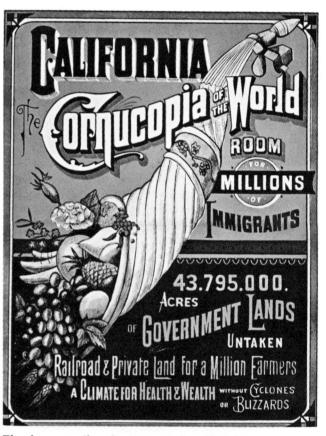

Flamboyant railroad posters of the 1880's left no uncertainties in readers' minds. The garish broadsides blanketed fences, barns, and railroad depots throughout the eastern half of the country. Thousands more were posted in European cities.

ery, climate, hunting, fishing, and boating, then devoted six hundred words of small type to a clinical account of the diseases that could be relieved by living there, including rheumatic proclivities, ozoena, aphonic consumption; the text also noted that there were "several pthisical incurables, whose lives were unquestionably prolonged by residence here."

Although the promotional din attracted a parade of newcomers, the great stampede did not start until 1887, when the Santa Fe Railway reached Los Angeles and opened a rate war with the Southern Pacific. Up to then, transcontinental fares had been high enough to discourage many Easterners from migrating. Fares from the Missouri Valley, averaging about $125 at the start of the battle, began to cascade downward in a chain of reductions, reaching a low of one dollar, then leveled off at $25 for several months. For a time, transcontinental tickets were cheaper than short-run fares, and people living along the lines of the battling railroads bought long-distance tickets for short trips. As one historian noted, it was cheaper to visit California than to read about it.

As the trainloads pulled into Los Angeles, bringing one thousand, then two thousand, and finally five thousand persons a week, Southern California found itself suddenly short of hotels, homes, and schools. Many of the newcomers arrived with modest capital and they bought property for homes, businesses, and farms. Under mounting pressure, the demand for land escalated and soon exploded into the Great Boom.

Professional boomers, scenting prey, trooped in from the Middle West and helped boost the boom to an ever-increasing frenzy. With the cunning naïveté of the times, they resorted to a variety of devices to inveigle purchasers into investing. Brass bands, street processions, free excursions, free lunches, lotteries, balloon ascensions, and effulgent advertising carried the day. Developers of Coronado promised lot buyers one year's free supply of water and a monthly allotment of street-railway and ferry tickets.

Land was recklessly subdivided, some of it on inaccessible sites, and sold on option to the highest bidder. Tracts formerly used for sheep ranches and grain fields, and even orange groves, were cut up into town lots. The price of lots in Los Angeles rose from $500 in 1886 to $5000 the next year, and nearby ranchlands increased in value 1500 per cent in the same period. Between 1880 and 1890, the assessed valuation of Los Angeles rose from $5,000,000 to $45,000,000 and the county from $14,000,000 to $60,000,000. In the same decade, San Diego leaped from $600,000 assessed value to nearly $15,000,000, and the county increased twelvefold. Population likewise increased. Los Angeles rose from 11,000 in 1880 to a peak of 80,000 in 1888, then settled back to 50,000. San Diego jumped from 2600 to 16,000 in the same period. Growth throughout the Southland was not so dramatic, but still substantial. All of the other counties at least doubled in population.

The excitement could not be sustained indefinitely, however, and the boom subsided in 1889, leaving behind some well-rooted towns and subdivisions and a mass of empty promises. In Los Angeles County alone, sixty boom towns covering 125 square miles had a total population in 1889 of only 3350 souls. Some of the largest of the paper towns had no inhabitants at all, and two had only one resident apiece—a caretaker for a defunct hotel. The majority of the townsites returned to acreage, where "the plowshare passes over their ruins, and barley grows in the deserted streets."

Fortunately, the end of the Great Boom turned out to be less of a catastrophe than anyone had expected. Thanks to the conservative lending policies of the banks—which ended up with only 25 per cent of their capital in real estate loans—the boom expired without damaging the economy of Southern California. When it was over, the six southern counties found themselves with a score of promising new towns, and with more schools, business structures, roads, and electric railways than before. A host of industrious newcomers had become permanent residents, rural lands were being more fully and better utilized, and diversification of crops was well under way. Furthermore, the increase in population coupled with a solid agricultural economy enabled the whole of the Southland for the first time to approach political parity with Northern California, which had heretofore domineered in the state's affairs.

Invitation to Paradise

In an unparalled promotional outburst, the railroads inundated the rest of the world with a flood of books, articles, brochures, and organized letter-writing campaigns that extolled California's faultless climate ("tonic for healthy and tubercular alike"), spectacular scenery, recreational facilities, and money-making opportunities.

Posters, billboards, car cards, and exhibits assaulted the eye with a garish mishmash of fruit, vegetables, contented cattle, noble Indians, and the waterfalls of Yosemite. Lecturers showed colored lantern slides on the Chautauqua circuit; landscape artists exhibited enormous paintings of California scenery in Eastern exhibit halls. Every bookstore sold boxed sets of California stereopticon views, accordion-pleated sets of photographs, and giant picture books too large to hold on one lap.

Railroad promotion continued well into the early 1900's, as evidenced by this crowd of prospective colonists in London's Royal Galleries waiting for the slide lecture to begin at a special exhibit sponsored by Western railroads in 1909.

Yosemite's waterfalls and cliffs were exploited from the start as an attraction to tourists and settlers. The grandeur of the scenery inspired the foremost landscape painters of the day, such as Thomas Hill, whose dramatic canvases of Yosemite exhibited in the East helped draw people West.

California-bound settlers crowd the relatively sumptuous depot in Omaha during a lunch stop. As they continued westward, they would find the infrequent stations increasingly primitive, the food progressively less edible.

A Gentle and Easy Amble

The second human tidal wave to hit California came by train, starting in the 1870's. The tedious overland ride, akin to a sea voyage in duration and monotony, was portrayed in railroad promotion as a "gentle and easy amble," a sort of prolonged picnic shared with congenial folk.

In actuality, the emigrant trains were bleak, dirty, and glacially slow—one step up from the Conestoga that had carried previous generations West. Passengers brought their own bedding and food and lived in the coaches, preparing meals on cookstoves provided by the railroad. Occasionally, the trains were side-tracked to make way for fast freight or passenger expresses; sometimes they were left on sidings for days at a time.

No matter. The newcomers arrived in the state somewhat the worse for wear but eager to start a new life in the earthly paradise.

Hot, crowded, squalid emigrant trains creeping across the plains were a striking contrast to the cheery picture of overland train travel portrayed by the railroads' inspired promotional writers.

Emigrant tickets were sold one-way only, sometimes in combination with options to buy California real estate. Special fares were well below standard charges and were depressed even lower by a rate war.

Issued by CHICAGO, R. ISLAND & PACIFIC R. R.

SPECIAL EMIGRANT TICKET.

Chicago to SAN FRANCISCO

GOOD FOR

One EMIGRANT Passage.

(IN EMIGRANT CARS ONLY.)

Only on presentation of this Ticket, with Checks attached, and good only for 20 days from date.

CONDITIONS--In consideration of this ticket being sold by the C. R. I & P. R. R. at a reduced price from the regular first class rate it is hereby understood and agreed-upon by the purchaser, that it will be good for passage if presented within twenty (20) days (only) from *April, 14.* ....18__ after which time it will be void.

Jfohn

General Ticket Agent.

104

SAN FRANCISCO.

Issued by CHICAGO, ROCK ISLAND & PACIFIC RAILROAD. CENTRAL PACIFIC R. R.

Good in Emigrant Cars Only

UNION JUNCTION TO SAN FRANCISCO.

No Stop-Over Check will be given on this Ticket.

E 931 | This Check not good if detached. | EMIGRANT

104

Designed to be "the talk of the Western world," the great wedding-cake Hotel Del Coronado (1888) covered seven and a half acres, had 750 rooms, most of them with fireplaces and wall safes, an 11,000-square-foot ballroom, thirty billiard tables (four for ladies), and four bowling alleys. Caught in the collapse of the boom, it was saved by a deathbed infusion of capital. It is still in use.

"Finest Resorts in the World"

In the boom years, the stature of a city was often judged by the size and opulence of its leading hotels. Real estate developers included them in their propaganda, often promoting them with equal fervor as tourist stopovers or as sanitariums.

Scores of the promised hotels never got beyond the drawings in the brochures and many that did succumbed to bankruptcy. Some of the derelicts were taken over by fledgling colleges. Pomona started its career in abandoned Hotel Claremont (renamed Sumner Hall) in 1888; and La Verne acquired the grotesque Lordsburg Hotel in 1889.

The luxury hotels that actually opened their doors and weathered the boom's collapse became internationally known for luxury and service. Most notable of these: Monterey's Del Monte (1880), the Arlington, in Santa Barbara (1886), Pasadena's Raymond and Green hotels (1886), and the one-and-only Hotel Del Coronado (1888).

"Crocker's Folly," the Hotel Del Monte, was one of the earliest of the boom caravansaries. Built on sand dunes in 1880 by the Central Pacific to attract wealthy and fashionable travelers, it confounded the carpers by succeeding from the start. It featured 126 acres of landscaped gardens, a race track, and a cypress maze. Rooms had hot and cold water even on the top floors, and telephone lines to the stables. Swept by fire in 1887, it was rebuilt more luxuriously than before. (It burned again in 1924 and was replaced with the present structure.)

Monterey, California.

America's Famous Summer and Winter Resort.

"Where a leaf never dies in the still blooming bowers,
And the bee banquets on thro' a whole year of flowers."

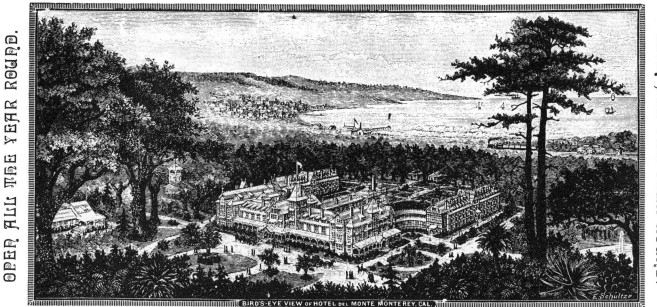

BIRD'S-EYE VIEW OF HOTEL DEL MONTE MONTEREY, CAL.

THE CELEBRATED
HOTEL DEL MONTE,

"The Queen of American Watering Places" and **"The Most Elegant Seaside Establishment in the World."**

TERMS FOR BOARD : { By the Day, $3.00 and Upward.
Parlors from $1.00 to $2.50 per Day, Extra.
Children in Children's Dining Room, $2.00 per day.

For further information address
GEO. SCHÖNEWALD, Manager,
Monterey. Cal,

Millionaires for the Day

Free food appears to have been in the inducement that drew bidders to this open-air auction at Montrose in 1890. Under the pounding spell of the auctioneer, buyers would lose all grip on credibility and bid thousands for land purchased for hundreds. Not all real estate was sold so openly, however, and many buyers blindly purchased lots that they had never seen on mountain peaks, under water, at the bottom of ravines, or in desert wastes.

Exhilaration of the Great Outdoors

"Come to the Campers' Paradise!" exhorted a railroad advertisement for the Santa Cruz Mountains, where there is "Grand Scenery, Fine Fishing, Good Hunting, Lovely Flowers, Grateful Shade, and No Mosquitos."

Boom-time promoters lost no time in reaching outdoor lovers with the story of the state's scenic and recreational enticements. In 1872, writer Charles Nordhoff described an encounter with "two square miles of geese" so tame that they took flight only after he had ridden into the flock. Earlier, publicist James Hutchings portrayed the delights of camping in Yosemite and hunting in Mariposa Grove, where he and a companion met a grizzly. " 'Hold, Mr. C., if you please—let us have the first shot at that immense fellow there.' 'With pleasure,' was the reply."

In the 1860's, skiers were blazing speed records in the Sierra; many of the peaks in the High Country had been scaled by 1875; and by 1890, hunters had succeeded in eradicating whole species of game animals and birds.

Pioneer campers pitched tents in the mountains from 1850's on. First campers on Mount Wilson behind Pasadena lit bonfires as a signal of arrival.

Two daredevil maidens kick up their heels in 1890 on the Overhanging Rock on Glacier Point, a mile straight up from the hard floor of Yosemite Valley. This giddy outcrop attracted showoffs for years before it was fenced off. While still accessible, it served as a stage for handstands, photographers, riders on horseback, and even an early Studebaker car.

Norwegian miners introduced ski-racing in the Sierra in 1850's, mostly for wagers. Annual winter sports events, started in 1860, ran for several years.

Natural wonders converted to curiosities by man's manipulations have also drawn their share of visitors to the outdoors. The famous drive-through tree in the Mariposa Grove bemused three generations of travelers after it was tunneled out in 1881. It fell in 1969.

A College in Every Town

One sure enticement for buyers of real estate was the promise of a college to be built in a proposed boom town. "College Town" implied solidity and security, and promoters offered colleges, seminaries, technical schools, and universities in profusion. Most of the dream schools never got beyond the artist's rendering in the brochures, a few opened their doors for a semester or two, and a handful miraculously survived.

A half-dozen private colleges and universities in the Los Angeles area owe their existence to the Great Boom. The University of Southern California, the California Institute of Technology, Pomona, Occidental, Redlands, Whittier, and La Verne all were launched on the sea of real estate profits in the late 1880's—and all of them suffered near-fatal disaster when the excitement subsided. With their endowments frozen in depressed real estate, their benefactors stripped of funds, and their students too impoverished to pay tuition and subsistence fees, the institutions were cruelly beset. How they managed to survive is a study in legerdemain that still bemuses historians.

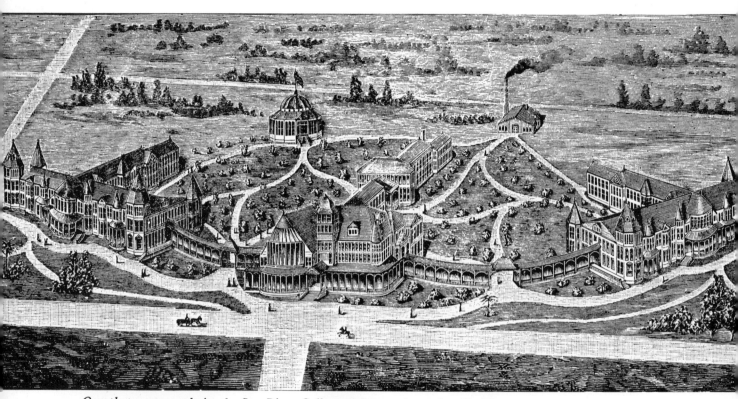

One that never made it: the San Diego College of Letters, located at Pacific Beach, opened promisingly in 1888 with one completed building on its seventeen-acre campus. It offered three courses of study—classical, scientific, and literary—and lasted three semesters. It expired with the end of the boom, and its lone building became a hotel.

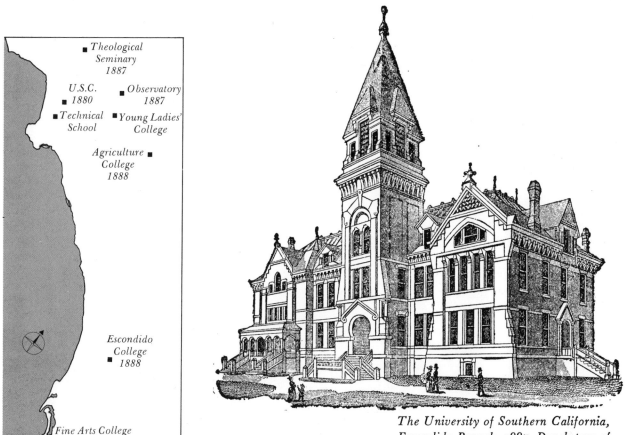

The University of Southern California, Escondido Branch, 1887. Developers of the town of Escondido offered U.S.C. a $250,000 land endowment for a college and erected the $40,000 structure above just in time for collapse of the boom. Never opened to college students, it became a grammar and high school.

When U.S.C. was literally the University of Southern California, in 1888, the school's far-flung units were scattered all over Southern California. Starting in 1880, the university invested profits from a lucrative real estate venture into forming a great "University System" with specialized branches. By 1888, it had five campuses in operation, two in prospect. The imperial dream capsized with the end of the boom. In 1893, U.S.C. had only twenty-five students. Recovery was excruciatingly slow and painful.

Launching of Occidental College in 1887 depended on a real estate promotion. The "university" secured a donation of fifty acres of land east of Los Angeles and put most of it up for sale. Opened in 1888, the school was nearly bankrupted a year later by the boom's collapse. Only the steadfast support of the Presbyterian Church saved it from extinction, enabled it in time to become one of the most prosperous of the privately endowed colleges on the coast.

"Wines Beyond Compare"

Oldest of California crops, wine grapes were introduced by the padres at Mission San Gabriel in 1771 and were soon planted at every mission to provide sacramental and drinking wine. The wine was heavy and bitter, but it was the only kind available in Spanish-Mexican California for sixty years. When the first American vineyards were planted, they were set out with mission cuttings. Later winegrowers imported more palatable varieties from Europe and the tart mission grapes gradually vanished from the vineyards.

As part of an agricultural boom in the 1870's, thousands of acres of vineyard were planted. Plantings ran as high as twenty-five million acres in a year, and some vineyards sold for two thousand dollars an acre. There was a ready demand for the wines. One reporter noted in 1872 that there were no three-year-old wines in the state and "the wine-maker sells his wine as fast as he can make it."

A Frenchman's acerbic view of wine pressing in California, reproduced in Harper's Illustrated Weekly *in 1878, shows Chinese trampling out the vintage —a personal touch that the industry later dispensed with.*

BACCHUS IN AMERICA—THE OLD WINE GOD AND THE NEW.

Allegorical poster of the 1870's portrays a joyous happening in Yosemite Valley, celebrating the notion that California's wines had caught up to European vintages in quality.

The label for a bottle of "rare old sauterne"—probably aged all of two months—typified the vintners' custom of attaching European varietal names to California wines to give them prestige, even though the local wines tasted nothing like their classic namesakes.

Neat, manicured groves of fragrant citrus spread for miles, surrounding and isolating the growers' mansions in an ocean of trees (left). Citrus growing brought to Southern California a modified plantation culture, operated by gentleman farmers. The fruit was crated for shipping in packing sheds (right) run by growers' associations.

Romance of the Orange

As venerable as the wine industry, citrus growing was rooted in the mission plantings of the late 1700's, and the first commercial groves were set out in the 1850's with cuttings from mission trees. The fruit was no match for that shipped in from Hawaii and Central America, however, and the industry languished. As a writer noted in 1875, the California orange was at that time "thick-skinned, sour, pithy, and dry . . . an insult to the noblest of fruit. . . . The lemons, great overgrown things, with skin half an inch thick, over a dry spongy interior, were more worthy of pity than contempt."

This dour picture was immeasurably brightened in 1873 by the introduction of a new variety, the Washington navel orange, which was flavorful, juicy, and durable enough to survive long-distance shipping. It launched a citrus boom, and by 1889 there were thirteen thousand acres growing in the six southern counties alone, the industry was valued at more than two million dollars, and new groves were being planted in spite of the subsidence of the great real estate boom.

Problems involved in shipping a spoilable commodity great distances dogged the industry in its early years, but were finally solved by the creation of growers' marketing co-operatives, most notably the California Fruit Growers Exchange (1895), famed for its ubiquitous trademark, *Sunkist*.

Production from the individual groves was identified by colorful box labels (below), for many years a bright spot in the corner grocery. Growers went to extravagant lengths to establish brand identification, as the sampling shows. Other favored symbols: flowers, heroes, historic events, famous places, pretty girls, military hardware, and the growers' children, pets, and wives.

1900-1920

New Century-New Order

WITHIN the opening decades of the new century, California came of age. For better or worse, the idiosyncrasies that now distinguish it from other states became firmly established, and most of the problems that still beset the state made their first appearances before World War I.

By 1900, the young state had enjoyed a half century of rapid but uneven growth. The final ripening was nurtured by the emergence of Southern California from an agricultural community to a commercial-industrial complex capable of challenging the bastions of industry and finance in the north. With a few notable exceptions, most of the events that had state-wide significance in the early 1900's occurred outside the San Francisco region.

The rapid growth of Southern California had continued after the Great Boom, and the influx of settlers proceeded without letup, in spite of short-lived panics, booms, and busts, filling out the southern counties and helping to build the new industrial complex.

A fortuitous combination turned the south to industry. Discovery of an abundance of oil in the 1890's together with the subsequent opening of new markets for petroleum products established a new basic industry and attracted satellite businesses. Previously handicapped by lack of coal, the tradi-

Crowds gather before the forty-four-story Tower of Jewels in 1915 on dedication day of the Panama-Pacific International Exposition. The opulent fair, which celebrated California's admittance to world commerce, also marked the end of an age of innocence, then drawing to a close on the battlefields of Europe.

tional industrial fuel, the Southland could now offer fuel oil and later electric power as clean, cheap, and flexible substitutes. In addition, ample land was available for factories of any size, and the benign climate permitted plants to operate all year without shutdowns for ice or snow. An ironic side benefit of San Francisco's tragic earthquake of 1906 was a temporary migration of business away from the quake-stricken north to the south.

The late emergence of the Southland as an industrial complex brought untold advantages to local entrepreneurs. Lacking fixed traditions, businessmen were free to experiment with new industrial processes, even some that conservative bankers viewed askance. The disreputable nickelodeon of the penny arcade became transformed into the giant and respected movie industry. The madmen assembling frail flying machines in barns and abandoned churches, found themselves with more orders than they could handle, literally standing on the ground floor of the Air Age. The names of the pioneer manufacturers soon became flying trademarks: Martin, Douglas, Lockheed, Vultee, Curtiss, and Ryan. Stimulated by military orders in World War I, the industry expanded, then slumped after the armistice, only to rebound a generation later.

Appearance of the prolific motorcar gave a further boost to the Southland's economy by providing a new customer for petroleum products, abetting the spread of the cities to the suburbs, and influencing the design of highway systems and subdivision layouts. Los Angeles was the first major city in the world to mature after the arrival of the automobile, and much of its character was shaped by the new mobility.

As new industries developed, additional outlets for their growing production became imperative, and the coast launched a port-building boom, accelerated by the dazzling benefits that were expected to accrue from the opening of the Panama Canal. San Diego hopefully dredged its harbor in 1914, Los Angeles poured millions into converting the mud flats of San Pedro into a first-class port, and Long Beach built a port to compete with San Pedro. In the north, the San Francisco Bay region hustled to protect its long maritime monopoly. San Francisco expanded dock facilities along the Embarcadero, Oakland began driving piles, and Sacramento and Stockton increased their facilities.

The long-awaited completion of the Panama Canal was understandably greeted with jubilation, symbolized by twin expositions in 1915 in San Diego and San Francisco. The "wedding of the oceans" more than halved the sailing time and distance between the two coasts and shortened the sea lanes to the east coast of Latin America.

Along with its consolidation as an industrial and commercial power, California witnessed a corresponding growth in organized labor—fought every inch of the way by organized management.

The north, having started as a commercial center, developed a strong union movement early in the 1860's. By 1900, unions were universally recognized and closed-shop contracts were accepted in many industries. However, a prolonged, dog-eat-dog struggle between labor and management over the closed shop in 1900 resulted in a setback for the exclusive contract. In 1901, another bitter struggle ensued over unionization of street railway workers. This strike had political overtones and it resulted in the unseating of a reform mayor, James D. Phelan, who had been cornered into taking an unpopular stand. Most celebrated of the labor causes, of course, was the "martyrdom" of Thomas Mooney and Warren Billings, convicted of bombing a Preparedness Day parade in 1916. As many labor sympathizers believed they had been railroaded, the pair's imprisonment provided a symbol of labor oppression that lasted for years.

If the northern businessman could occasionally tolerate a closed-shop contract, there were few if any who would bow to one in Southern California.

By tradition agriculturally oriented, the area was already unfriendly to organized labor when industrialization arrived in the 1890's. From 1900 on, labor organizers somehow managed to attract hundreds of members, but the unions had little bargaining power and could rarely breach the monolithic front of organized management. Provocateurs attempted to break management's commitment to the open shop in 1910 and 1911, but their tactics served only to solidify the opposition. Climax of the unions' blundering came with the tragic dynamiting of the Los Angeles *Times,* bull-horn voice of the open shop, which resulted in Southern California's rigid commitment to the open shop for thirty years.

Keeping pace with industrial development, agricultural growth had settled down by 1900 into a recognizable pattern. California farming had acquired two notable characteristics: it was being conducted on a grand scale and it was producing an amazing diversity of crops.

Large-scale farms, hand-me-downs from the huge Mexican land grants, required gargantuan machines, armies of stoop labor, and princely expenditures of capital. The scope of the operations placed ownership in the hands of large corporations, whose impersonal attitude toward the field workers, mostly ethnic minorities, sometimes provoked conflict when grievances were presented. Beginning in Wheatland in 1913, strikes, riots, and lockouts have been an all-too-frequent feature of the harvest season.

The diversity in agricultural production was simply a reflection of California's natural variety in climate, soils, and topography. By 1900, the era of extravagant experiment was over. No longer would farmers gamble on plantings of tobacco, tea, coffee, bananas, mangoes, and other exotics. Experimental work was taken over by the state agriculture service and the "cow college" at Davis. Farmers were left free to cope with variety enough to please any would-be Burbank: avocados, pomegranates, dates, olives, citrus in variety, and grapes. Vineyards blanketed thousands of acres, producing both table and wine grapes in abundance. Nearly wiped out by a plague of phylloxera, viticulture was on solid footing by 1900. The state's vineyards accounted for more than 80 per cent of the national output of wines, and California vintages were being savored the world over.

The agricultural abundance could never have occurred if a plentiful supply of water had not been secured. Local sources were taxed to the limit by 1900, and parched cities and agricultural districts banded together to import water hundreds of miles from the Sierra, Colorado River, or Northern California rivers.

The reach for water proved from the start to be a prickly political nettle. Residents in water-rich areas resisted the "grab" by the water-poor, and the water programs were characterized by sulfurous acrimony, interminable litigation, and sabotage. The disputes have long since been decently buried, but a residue of rancor still exists in some quarters.

The quest for water goes on today as the need continues to grow. Desalination plants off the coast of Los Angeles are pumping purified sea water into metropolitan mains, and engineers are combing the mountains for possible damsites.

In its political development, the state had adopted postures by 1900 that persist to this day. For forty years after admission, political power rested with the mining counties of the north, and the cow counties of the south had little leverage. Growth of the south eased this imbalance somewhat, but even now the rural constituencies possess a pivotal hold on legislation.

In the 1900's, political morality was at a low ebb. The state had gotten off to an unfortunate start in the 1850's. Left to its own devices by Congress for nearly two years, the state government was spawned without either traditions or controls. Furthermore, the skylarking attitude of the forty-niners did not contribute to development of sterner political virtues. As a consequence, government was riddled with corruption for years. Periodic reform movements shook one set of rascals out of one city hall after another only to make room for another group of the same ilk. Massive graft trials in San Francisco in 1906 brought a parade of culprits to justice, but the ramifications of evil-doing were so widespread that respectable citizens found themselves implicated, and they dropped their backing of the reformers. Of the four-hundred-odd persons indicted, four were convicted, and only one imprisoned.

Contributing to the debacle was the inimitable

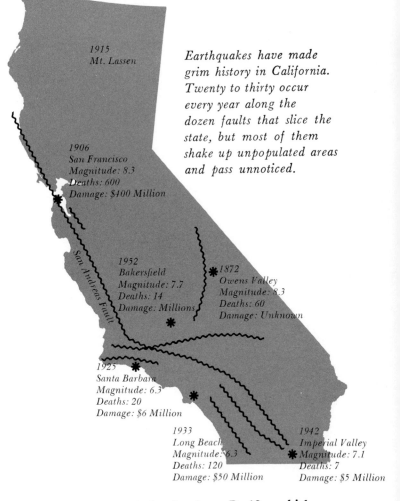

Earthquakes have made grim history in California. Twenty to thirty occur every year along the dozen faults that slice the state, but most of them shake up unpopulated areas and pass unnoticed.

1915
Mt. Lassen

1906
San Francisco
Magnitude: 8.3
Deaths: 600
Damage: $400 Million

San Andreas Fault

1952
Bakersfield
Magnitude: 7.7
Deaths: 14
Damage: Millions

1872
Owens Valley
Magnitude: 8.3
Deaths: 60
Damage: Unknown

1925
Santa Barbara
Magnitude: 6.3
Deaths: 20
Damage: $6 Million

1933
Long Beach
Magnitude: 6.3
Deaths: 120
Damage: $50 Million

1942
Imperial Valley
Magnitude: 7.1
Deaths: 7
Damage: $5 Million

political machine of the Southern Pacific, which carried on a shadow government that operated with more efficiency and, by the company's lights, more honor than the constituted authorities. Public opposition to the tie-up between the lax public officials and the powerful corporation eventually resulted in electing a reform governor, Hiram Johnson, who pledged to free the state of the railroad's grip. Actually, the grip had long since been loosened by competition from other railroads that had broken the company's monopoly. At any rate, the company was content to get out of politics and let the new governor take credit for slaying the dragon. Johnson introduced a number of overdue reforms in the state government, most of them not related to the railroad, and California began to benefit from a more wholesome political climate.

OVERLEAF: *A dramatic painting by marine artist W. A. Coulter captures the agony of the "bonny, merry city" of San Francisco on the first day of its ordeal by fire following the earthquake of 1906. The artist shows North Beach and Telegraph Hill in flames and the impromptu flotilla of watercraft that ferried refugees to safety across the bay.*

Businessmen open safes left closed for several days after the fire to prevent the superheated contents from disintegrating in a puff of ash when exposed to the air. Earthquake damage (below) in San Francisco was severest on filled ground.

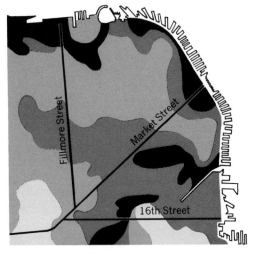

Trial by Fire

On a never-to-be-forgotten morning in April 1906 the San Andreas Fault fractured along a 240-mile path and inflicted the most devastating earthquake in the state's history, killing several hundred persons and destroying millions of dollars' worth of property in Northern California.

The effects of the disaster reached far beyond the immediate damage. For a time, newcomers to the state shunned the San Francisco Bay Area and settled in "stabler" Southern California, and industries planning to come West likewise gravitated south. Building codes were tightened throughout the state to make future construction more earthquake resistant, and plans were developed to insure that later quakes would not take such a toll as this one. Severe earthquakes occurring since have revealed that not every city has read the lessons in San Francisco's tragic experience—perhaps not even San Francisco itself.

Stanford Memorial Chapel, nearly destroyed by the earthquake, was typical of some of the damage suffered along the length of the fault from Fort Ross to Hollister. East Bay cities, on a different fault system, escaped major damage.

*In an early use of fire hoses to disperse rioters, police
flush members of the International Workers of the
World off the streets of San Diego in 1911. The
anarchistic I.W.W.'s, opposed to both capital and
labor, fomented discord in Fresno and San Diego
for eight months. The Wobblies' activist message was
broadcast by means of stickers (below) posted on
letters, parcels, telephone poles.*

Militant Labor

Open shop or closed shop? The choice facing labor and
management in the early 1900's became more and more
meaningful as the state's industrial growth accelerated.

Commitment to one or the other of these opposing
philosophies early took on a regional character. The closed
shop had long been accepted in San Francisco by virtue
of its rapid growth into a commercial, shipping, and industrial center. By 1900, organized labor was powerful
enough to elect its own mayor.

By contrast, Southern California was an unfriendly place
for the closed shop. With a brand new and widely dispersed
industrial complex that was not bound by any traditions
in labor relations, the Southland was a natural center for
the open shop, and Los Angeles was its capital and Mecca.

Labor tried to buck the setup in the south and scores
of unions were organized after 1900, but few of them
secured closed-shop contracts. The movement was se-
verely handicapped by radical activists and by the senseless
bombing of the Los Angeles *Times*.

Citadel of the open shop in Los Angeles, the Times, *was dynamited in 1910 by a professional union saboteur, J. J. McNamara, member of a conspiratorial team assigned to disintegrate opponents of organized labor in the area. McNamara's time bomb, placed among ink barrels next to the building, destroyed the plant in an appalling inferno that killed twenty-one employees. In the course of a tense and dramatic trial that attracted international attention, the accused unexpectedly confessed guilt, thereby stunning his supporters and setting the cause of organized labor in the area back a generation. Los Angeles remained an open-shop city for thirty years afterward.*

The Reach for Water

To slake the thirst of its burgeoning cities located hundreds of miles from natural sources of water, California has five times engaged in massive water programs that have involved great engineering prowess and political sagacity.

First of the giant reach-outs, Los Angeles' Owens River Aqueduct (1907–13) was an astonishing construction feat, but it was embroiled in bitter controversy from the start. Residents around the Sierra intake battled for years for reparations for confiscated property. Residents at the spigot end of the pipe line were nettled to find that their bond money had brought water only to the outskirts. They had to vote more millions to bring it to the city's mains.

When San Francisco went to the mountains for water, it too ran into contention. The city chose one of the grandest of the Sierra canyons for a reservoir site and touched off a fight with conservationists that raged for years and reached all the way to the White House before it was settled in favor of the city in 1913.

The first rush of Owens River water from the Sierra 240 miles away cascades down spillway on the outskirts of Los Angeles before an excited crowd in 1913. Not so jubilant, residents of Owens Valley resented confiscation of their land, later (1923–24) dynamited the pipe line (above), cutting off water for a million Angelenos.

A crushing defeat for conservationists led by John Muir was the taking of the Grand Canyon of the Tuolumne (above) for the Hetch Hetchy reservoir (right) to serve San Francisco. The battle raged for eight years, led to founding of the militant Sierra Club.

Sweeping Back the Flood

Before it was filled with water, the canyon of the Tuolumne nearly equaled the grandeur of the famous Merced Canyon in Yosemite a few miles to the south. Conservationists contended that less scenic areas would have served.

Water for the Desert

It took unfettered imagination to visualize crops growing in the alkaline wastes of the Imperial Valley, and the handful of men who promoted the notion campaigned fruitlessly for decades before securing the necessary capital.

The promoters were confident that, once irrigation water reached the valley, the natural fertility of the soil would yield an abundance. When the dream was finally accomplished, the reality outstripped the vision. The mild winter climate stimulated crops to ripen weeks or even months before they matured elsewhere, thus giving the farmers a jump on the market. Within a few years, the valley was checkerboarded with croplands, citrus groves, and date plantations, and the area became one of the world's most fruitful gardens. At present, more than three thousand miles of canals serve five hundred thousand cultivated acres and a dozen major cities.

(a) Original Form

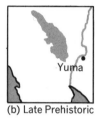
(b) Late Prehistoric

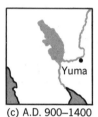
(c) A.D. 900–1400

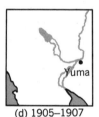
(d) 1905–1907

Out in the middle of nowhere in 1901, a farmer turns Colorado River water into his irrigation ditches. Reclamation of the Salton Sink was the culmination of forty years of agitation.

Imperial Valley's off-and-on sea was originally (a) part of the Gulf of California that once stretched as far north as San Gorgonio Pass. A silt dam formed at the mouth of the Colorado River (b) cut the gulf in two and created a salt-water sea. The sea dried up, only to be refilled (c) when the river changed its course. In its turn, this body of water evaporated, leaving behind the Salton Sink, which the first settlers began to reclaim in 1901. A break in a canal (d) formed the present Salton Sea in 1905-7.

Unexpected and unwelcome, a torrent of water poured into the Imperial Valley in 1905 through a gap in a Colorado River canal below the border. Fed by heavy snows in the Rockies, the rampaging river refilled an ancient sea and submerged croplands and the Southern Pacific's main line to New Orleans. On its own, the railroad closed the gap with rock in a costly two-year struggle.

For many years, the industry was restricted to outdoor shooting because of the slowness of the films then available. Even indoor scenes were shot outdoors in strong sunlight. The fields around Hollywood were filled in with standing sets, such as this vintage piece for Douglas Fairbanks' Thief of Bagdad.

Teasers for next week's feature were flashed on the screens of the early movies, interspersed with admonitions about removing hats and not expectorating on the floor.

Sunshine Industry

Outgrowth of the five-cent peep show, the movie industry got its start in California in 1908, when public clamor for the "flickers" attracted dozens of self-made producers, most of whom were fugitives from an Eastern syndicate that controlled the basic patents on the new industry and exacted tribute for every film. Safe for a time in the slumbering suburbs of Los Angeles, they cranked out a spate of one-reel Westerns and comedies.

The flight to California turned out to have advantages beyond temporary security from the syndicate, which soon moved here too. The climate permitted a longer season for outdoor shooting and more days of sunshine for the slow films of the time; and, as a special bonus, the geographic diversity of the state duplicated the world's scenery within a radius of a few miles. Once started, the industry ballooned into one of the state's leading income producers.

Before the era of the big star, film producers often impressed amateurs for bit parts and played them opposite well-known performers. Here, in a scene from a World War I tearjerker, Gladys Smith (just renamed Mary Pickford) bids good-by to Glenn L. Martin, in real life a local aircraft designer who later made a distinguished record as a manufacturer of bombers, flying boats (notably the China Clipper), and passenger planes.

A historic sequence of photos taken by Eadweard Muybridge in 1878 at the behest of Leland Stanford settled a $25,000 wager that a galloping horse would at some time have all four hoofs off the ground. With a set of twenty-four cameras tripped by wires, the photographer proved Stanford right and contributed to the early development of the movies.

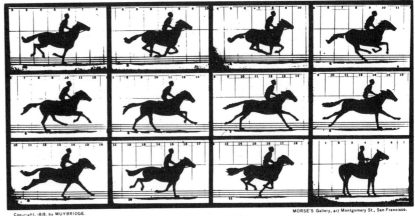

Copyright, 1878, by MUYBRIDGE.

THE HORSE IN MOTION.

MORSE'S Gallery, 417 Montgomery St., San Francisco.

*Preview of the coming Air Age, a massed flight of
212 warplanes over San Diego celebrates the end of
World War I. San Diego was major training center.*

Pioneers in Flight

"Viva aviation! May untoward circumstances never clip its
wings!" exclaimed the Los Angeles *Times* in 1910 at the
end of the nation's first air meet held nearby.

Portents of California's involvement with aviation appeared early. In 1883, the country's first glider-flight took
wing near San Diego, twenty years before the Wright
brothers' historic takeoff. Manufacturing on a cottage-
industry basis began in 1909, when Glenn Martin assembled his first plane in an abandoned church in Santa
Ana. Three years later, he flew a hydroplane to Santa
Catalina Island. In 1916, the Lockheed brothers introduced
their now famous name in Santa Barbara; and four years
later, another well-known family of planes was launched
by Donald Douglas, who pieced together his first transport
in a shack behind a Santa Monica barbershop.

Military aircraft became a familiar sight during World
War I, when hundreds of air cadets earned their wings in
the sunny skies over Southern California.

*FIRST AVIATION MEET in the
country was staged in Los Angeles in
1910, presaging the role that this
area was soon to play in its
development of the aircraft industry.*

Three eras of transportation: a Navy hydroplane flies over a steam sailing vessel in San Diego Bay in 1911. Development of the hydroplane was pioneered in this harbor, which was also the setting for world's first takeoff from a ship.

Discovery of oil in Los Angeles dirtied the face of the city. Hundreds of tarry derricks sprouted on Signal Hill (above), located over one of the richest oil pools in the country. No neighborhood was immune from oil fever, and when a producing well was brought in with a pick and shovel in 1893 in the downtown area, derricks blossomed (below) amid established residences.

Black Gold!

The discovery of oil in commercial quantities around the turn of the century had an explosive effect on the economy of Southern California, changing it from an agricultural to an industrial center and wracking it with recurrent financial crises.

As early as the 1850's, wildcatters had found oil in moderate amounts, adequate to sustain the modest market for asphalt, paraffin, and kerosene. But after 1900, one oil field after another blew in, and the oil companies found themselves literally wallowing in crude oil, which sometimes ran in the streets. So great was the demand for petroleum and the rush for drilling sites, that stock sharpsters enjoyed a bonanza. The industry was rocked with scandals. Stock promotions were over-sold—one involved the sale of 3,000,000 shares for a ghost company chartered at 600,000 —respectable bankers were ruined by speculative oil schemes, and at least one notable figure in the industry, Ed Doheny, was implicated in the Teapot Dome scandal.

The greatest gusher of all time, Lake View No. 1, in the San Joaquin Valley, broke loose in 1910, spewed out nine-million barrels of crude without letup for eighteen months, depressed the petroleum market.

Magic Spanish City

The gemlike replica of a Spanish-colonial city, planted full-blown on a sandy mesa in San Diego, was this city's way of heralding the completion of the Panama Canal in 1915. An "astounding feat"—in the words of Woodrow Wilson—for a city of seventy thousand, the Panama-California Exposition made no attempt to compete with the much larger show in San Francisco and limited itself to the culture of the Southwest.

The fair was a bold bid to attract commerce to San Diego. Leading citizens feared that the city's location in the southwesternmost corner of the country would cause it to be bypassed by new business generated by the opening of the canal. The exposition enticed people to come and see for themselves the manifold potentialities of "The First Port of Call." Unfortunately, although the fair drew 3,760,000 enchanted visitors, it failed to lure the hoped-for industries, and it is chiefly remembered for the charm of its setting and its architecture.

Designed "to link the spirit of the old seekers of the Eldorado with that of the Twentieth Century," Bertram Goodhue's baroque Spanish town was inspired by colonial architecture of Mexico, characterized by dramatic contrast of plain façades with richly ornamented window openings, doorways, towers, domes. San Diego's trademark, the California Building (right), was derived from Tepotzotlán Cathedral, pictured next to it, which is regarded as one of Mexico's finest examples of churrigueresque. The exposition stimulated a Spanish revival in the state, generated a host of Spanish-style buildings.

Massive exhibit halls, designed in a curious blend of Romanesque and Lost Atlantis architecture, were formally grouped around spacious squares, courts, sunken gardens, and promenades. At the conclusion of the exposition, some of the foreign exhibits were shipped to the San Diego fair, which continued for a second year, and all but a few of the buildings were demolished. A notable exception was the romantic Palace of Fine Arts, which was granted a reprieve to disintegrate slowly for a half century. It was restored in 1967.

A memorable innovation was a dazzling light show produced every night by a battery of searchlights manned by marines. The 3,600,000-candle-power scintillator swept the skies with every hue in the rainbow and could be seen as far away as Sacramento.

The World on View

San Franciscans had no doubts about the benefits that would accrue to their city from the shortened sea connection with the Atlantic, and they saluted the opening of the Panama Canal with a year-long fifty-million-dollar show.

The Panama-Pacific International Exposition, which opened a month after the San Diego fair, attracted exhibitors from twenty states and twenty-five foreign countries. Although half of the nations represented were already locked in mortal combat in Europe, their exhibits conveyed an eerie illusion of normalcy. Foreign exhibitors were given a free hand in the design of their pavilions, and they assembled a bewildering array of mosques, temples, windmills, and palaces. State pavilions, likewise left on their own, offered reproductions of such curiosities as George Washington's Trenton Barracks, a Fifth Avenue mansion, and, for California, a very synthetic mission.

A quaint art-nouveau postcard celebrates the elation felt by many people at the meeting of the two oceans via the Panama Canal.

Megalopolis on the Way

"People are fast filling the habitable parts of this southern land with homes as no other part of the world can show, and the end of their work no man can foresee." So wrote a prophetic observer in 1886 at the start of the great migration to Southern California; and in fulfillment of his prediction, waves of newcomers poured into the area, doubling the census every decade.

The horizontal spread that has since blanketed the southern part of the state was induced early in the 1900's by a combination of factors. The flat valley lands were easy to survey and subdivide, cheap to build on. As farms and orchards were absorbed by the spreading metropolis, particularly in the Los Angeles area, property was introduced on the market in large blocs, often of township or city scale. A proliferation of street railways and the automobile opened distant suburbs, often years ahead of population.

The early appearance of mass housing in San Francisco occurred in the 1870's, when hundreds of slim houses, decorated with bay windows and riotous scrollwork, were built in the Western Addition. The narrow twenty-five-foot lots, derived from the Spanish pueblo, lent themselves to jam-packed housing, and developers early adopted a style of cheek-by-jowl home construction that is still in practice.

By 1912, passengers ascending the sixty-two-degree cogwheel line up Mount Lowe could see the emerging pattern of Los Angeles, which already covered 108 square miles. The city's sprawling growth was abetted by three-story height limit imposed on buildings after the San Francisco quake and by a 1200-mile street railway net.

Los Angeles has expanded sixteenfold from the original pueblo of 1850. In 1906, a "shoestring" reached out to tidewater for port connections. The addition of San Fernando Valley in 1915 doubled the city's size. Present area: 450 square miles.

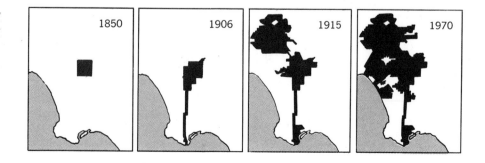

Californians Take the Wheel

The automobile found its natural habitat in California. The rapidly expanding state needed a means of transportation more flexible than the railways and less capricious than old Dobbin, and the motorcar took over the assignment with steadily increasing efficiency.

Touring clubs roamed the state in 1900, drumming up interest in road improvement. Oil companies started handing out road maps in 1910, and auto clubs began posting directional signs two years later. By 1910, there were thirty-six thousand cars registered in the state. Ten years later, the total had risen to six hundred thousand.

Although the governor could justify road improvements in 1907 only as a means to "save money in horse flesh, harness, wagons, and draught power," within two years the mapping of a complete state highway system was authorized and an appropriation of eighteen million dollars passed to construct paved roads. By 1920, an additional fifty-five million dollars had been spent, and the Automobile Age had arrived.

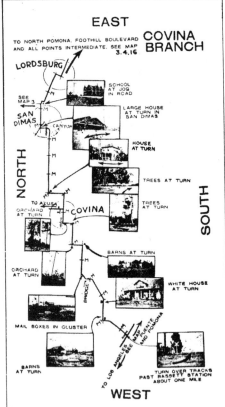

The first gas station maps relied on landmarks, as this 1910 handout from Union Oil illustrates. The state's first freeway (left), an elevated bikeway between Pasadena and Los Angeles, was started in 1900 but was never completed because of the opening of rail connections. The present freeway follows its path.

A procession of tin lizzies winds down a corkscrew grade east of San Diego in 1913
to publicize the opening of a new highway that was expected to draw traffic from
Imperial Valley to San Diego and away from Los Angeles. Unfortunately, the
tortuous upgrade proved a purgatory for the underpowered cars of the day, and
drivers avoided it in summer in favor of the longer but cooler route to Los Angeles.
Early highway development involved intense competition between cities.

Rapid transit in 1907.
Crowds wait to ride in an
experimental trolley that
whizzed for two miles
through Burbank orange
groves. The car was
whipped along at a brisk
clip by an airplane propeller
in its nose. Decades ahead of
its time, the imaginative
venture was abandoned for
lack of interested capital.

1920-1970

Patterns for Tomorrow

Since World War I, many events have made the headlines in California, but few have made history.

Between the two wars, the state moved sedately toward industrialization, with time out for the Depression. Waves of Dust Bowlers journeyed here in the thirties and settled in the agricultural valleys. A series of tantalizing political movements blossomed in Southern California, promising economic freedom to the old and the poor.

World War II emphatically committed the state to heavy industrial development. Aircraft factories and shipyards built up an enormous production, drawing many workers from out of state, mostly from the Deep South. Thousands of Negroes were recruited to work in war plants. Many returned home after the war, but the vast majority stayed on. The aircraft industry converted after the war to aerospace and continued its major role in the economy of the state.

During these years, Californians made their fateful compact with the automobile as their primary means of transport. The price for this commitment has been a pall of smog and a progressive strangulation of transportation in general.

Racial minorities, impatient with the glacial workings of due process, have attempted a short cut to a place in the sun by vigorously taking the initiative. A new breed of college students, replacing the goldfish eaters and the silent generation that slumbered through the classrooms of the 1950's, turned campuses into battlegrounds cementing conservative politicians into office.

A sharp rise in population brought about an acute housing shortage, which was solved with mass-produced subdivisions that spread urban boundaries to the horizon. Projects for the renewal of blighted urban cores began shaking the ground in the heart of every major city. Smaller communities planted grass in Main Street and renewed their aging downtown areas with beguiling malls.

Conservationists have made striking gains in adding new lands to the public domain, but they dare not relax their vigilance or lose their cunning, for they continue to face new land predators every day. Need for tougher controls over the exploitation of the state's natural resources has been revealed by a succession of catastrophes attributable to the ignorance or cupidity of oil drillers, subdividers, loggers, and resort developers.

California's recent history is inevitably part mirror image of what has been going on elsewhere, but the more significant events are those that reflect the truly unique aspects of the state or are the surfacings of historical currents that become visible here long before they reveal themselves in other parts of the country.

The following pages summarize some of the problems that California is solving for its own salvation, reviews some that are still unresolved. Hopefully, solutions to nagging urban crises to be worked out here may well show the way for the nation.

Pedestrians enjoy their one and only day on the Golden Gate Bridge, May 27, 1937. A link between eras, the stately span was conceived in 1917, surveyed the next year, and built during the Depression, 1933–37. Designed to carry vehicular traffic between San Francisco and the then sparsely settled Redwood Empire, the aerial freeway anticipated by several years the superhighways that now grid the state.

This all-too-familiar scene of rush-hour congestion on the freeways is sure to worsen as the torrent of vehicles continues to increase faster than road builders can accommodate it. Freeways require a decade from plan to ribbon cutting, and by the time a new one opens, it is liable to be obsolete.

Unsnarling the Traffic

In this state where every man is his own transit system, no other mode of transportation yet devised can equal the family car in meeting the needs of mobile Californians, who are inured to driving long distances, commuting 100 miles a day by car, and patronizing drive-in services ad infinitum.

With the car population growing as rapidly as the human birth rate in some parts of the state, however, the concentration of vehicles is escalating to the point where existing road systems will be unable to accommodate the wheeled horde. Introduction of a supplementary network is bound to come—despite the resourceful opposition of the automotive priesthood—and when it does, it will probably take the form of a family of complementary systems, each designed to serve a different need. Smogless transit systems of the 1980's are on the drawing boards, some are in the pilot stage, one is under way.

Captive four-passenger cars traveling on guideways are part of a future transportation system proposed by Stanford Research Institute. The scheme to move large masses of people swiftly, economically includes conveyor belts, automated cars, self-service electric carts, fast intercity links. All this by 1990.

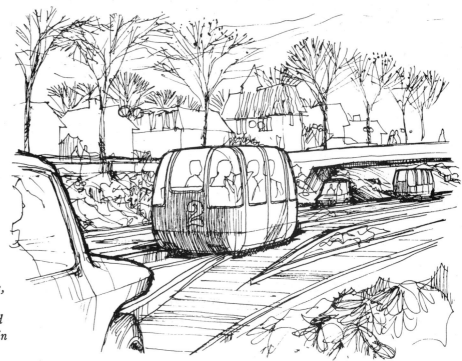

The first rapid transit system in the state, BART is designed to compete with automobiles in attractiveness, speed, and convenience, and to whisk commuters in electronically controlled trains at eighty miles an hour over elevated trackways, through tunnels, and under the mud of San Francisco Bay. Critics contend the system is already obsolete, will be an opulent white elephant. A similar scheme planned for metropolitan Los Angeles was voted down in 1968 by a slim margin.

A powerful transmitter in the Mojave Desert beams instructions to unmanned space vehicles, receives its cues from the Jet Propulsion Laboratory in Pasadena, an affiliate of Caltech. JPL also co-ordinates work of thousands of "cottage industries" that make watchlike parts for space vehicles.

Technology for Tomorrow

When the United States landed astronauts on the moon, much of their personal gear, the intricate hardware that got them there, and their instructions after they arrived came from California. Space Age technology accounts for a generous slice of the state's economic pie. In Los Angeles County alone, aerospace industries comprised 40 per cent of the industrial complex in 1968. A local concentration of technical colleges, aircraft plants, and think tanks makes Southern California a leader in the manufacture of space paraphernalia.

Curtailment of the space program by parsimonious administrations in Washington will compel the industry to shift to a host of related technologies, such as long-distance communications, weather satellites, deep-sea environments, automated transportation systems, nuclear power plants, desalination of sea water, and possibly, even earthquake prediction.

Moon suit: an experimental suit of armor for astronauts, designed by NASA's Ames Research Laboratory. All metal, with steel accordion pleats and ball-bearing joints, the suit protects astronauts against injury while prowling the moonscape. The suit was tested underwater to ascertain its airtightness.

After the SST, what? The HST, or
hypersonic transport, here shown
undergoing wind-tunnel tests at Ames
Research Laboratory. The craft will
whoosh passengers of the 1980's through
the air at five thousand miles per hour.
The design of the ship offers several
knotty problems: how to carry liquid
hydrogen fuel safely, what metal to use
for the air frame that will not burn up
at cruising speed, and how to shield
passengers from radiation given off by the
ship at top speed.

An aquanaut inspects happy-looking
submersible before it descends to a record
depth of 8310 feet. Deep Quest is one of a
school of research vessels built by airplane
makers for exploration of the ocean floor,
submarine rescue missions, and inspection
of underwater installations. The next
project: deep-sea housing.

The decaying produce center near San Francisco's waterfront was an unsanitary eyesore, too cramped for large-scale operations. Replaced by a modern complex in the outskirts, the district was razed in 1962 to make way for the Golden Gateway Redevelopment.

Humanizing Central City

Like cities everywhere, the major urban areas in California have been hurt by the flight from downtown to suburb, and they are industriously revitalizing their core areas to make them palatable to businessmen and residents alike. At their best, the new developments make sensible provision for open space around tall buildings, please the eye with ground-level landscaping, segregate automobile and pedestrian traffic, and make generous allowance for off-street parking.

The older cities have had to destroy and rebuild. In San Diego, an imaginative venture has reconstructed the old center of town into a metropolitan skyline; Los Angeles is slowly completing the Bunker Hill complex of business-residential structures; and San Francisco is well launched on an extravaganza of new office buildings, apartments, pedestrian malls, parks, and walk-through fountains.

Artful and thoughtful design contributes to the ingratiating atmosphere of the Golden Gateway residential development covering twenty square blocks in downtown San Francisco. Pedestrians are separated from automobiles by landscaped malls elevated to the second-story level (left) and connected by bridges that span the busy thoroughfares below, where shops and garages are located. A charming and immaculate park (right) features a wind-swept fountain, trees, and rolling hillocks of grass. The oasis attracts scores of brown-baggers from the financial district on summer noons.

The pent-up demand for housing after World War II caused mass construction on an unprecedented scale. Enormous subdivisions were knocked together in a remarkable concert of engineering and construction skills, but often with sketchy over-all planning and little concern for aesthetic niceties. Phenomenal Lakewood, on the outskirts of Long Beach, though built up from bean fields to a city of 17,500 homes in record time, was seemingly laid out with only a straightedge and a handful of house plans.

Housing for a New Day

The unremitting tide of newcomers that had been rolling into California for two generations swept to a new high during and after World War II, nearly doubling the state's population between 1940 and 1955. Housing for the incoming mass was grossly inadequate because of wartime restraints on home building. But once controls were lifted after the war, subdividers built endless rows of look-alike houses, mass-produced with breakneck speed. Many of these developments were well planned and attractively laid out, but scores were substandard or at best monotonous. For good or ill, they quickly sold out.

In the 1960's, construction of single-family dwellings slowed to a standstill, checked by rising land costs and taxes, overbuilding, and tight money. Builders turned to custom homes, cluster housing, or apartments, thereby setting a trend.

Typical of newer and more sensitive planning the apartment complex of Woodlake, near San Mateo, looks out on an artificial lake stocked with waterfowl and rimmed with attractive landscaping. The development stands next door to a freeway but seems remote from the frantic thoroughfare.

Low-rent housing can be as well designed and attractive as middle-income dwellings. This proposal for town-house clusters for San Francisco is based on a grouping of four to six houses around an entry garden court. Units can be spotted anywhere a site can be cleared.

Politics of Confrontation

In the mid-1960's, a wave of unrest began to roll over the state's campuses. A new breed of students, unafraid to challenge the ivy-encrusted administrations, adopted the techniques of the civil rights demonstrations to force action on their grievances and brought one college after another to a standstill. At the start, the issue was a meaningful rebellion against the punch-card impersonalization of the "multiversity." Later, the students vented their idealism in protesting the war in Vietnam, inequities in the draft, university involvement in weaponry research, and racial discrimination on campus.

Not all the issues were legitimate, nor were all the techniques of confrontation commendable, and the public reaction was clear and unequivocal. The fed-up voters swept into office conservative candidates pledged to end campus unrest, rejected bond issues for higher education, and demanded legislative discipline for activists.

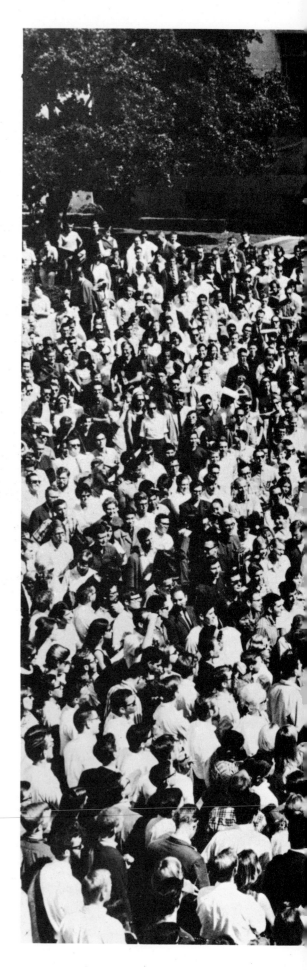

The start of it all. A student leader stands on the roof of a Berkeley police car and addresses a crowd of beardless, crew-cut U.C. students in 1964 during the Free Speech Movement. The car, which harbored an arrested student, was held captive by the crowd for eight hours. From this early challenge to established authority, other student revolts have followed on other campuses in other parts of the world.

The Battle of the Buttons. Like spring flowers, political lapel buttons come and go, proclaiming righteous and outrageous causes in terse and witty words. The goals shift year to year, month to month, day to day, and yesterday's buttons are often meaningless tomorrow.

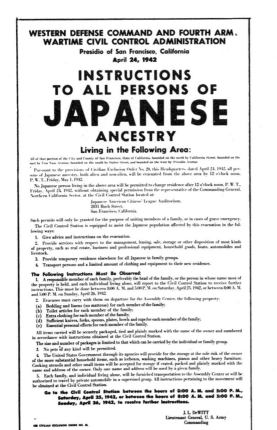

WESTERN DEFENSE COMMAND AND FOURTH ARM.
WARTIME CIVIL CONTROL ADMINISTRATION
Presidio of San Francisco, California
April 24, 1942

INSTRUCTIONS
TO ALL PERSONS OF
JAPANESE
ANCESTRY

Living in the Following Area:

All of that portion of the City and County of San Francisco, State of California, bounded on the north by California Street, bounded on the east by Van Ness Avenue, bounded on the south by Sutter Street, and bounded on the west by Presidio Avenue.

Pursuant to the provisions of Civilian Exclusion Order No. 20, this Headquarters, dated April 24, 1942, all persons of Japanese ancestry, both alien and non-alien, will be evacuated from the above area by 12 o'clock noon, P. W. T., Friday, May 1, 1942.

No Japanese person living in the above area will be permitted to change residence after 12 o'clock noon, P. W. T., Friday, April 24, 1942, without obtaining special permission from the representative of the Commanding General, Northern California Sector, at the Civil Control Station located at:

Japanese American Citizens' League Auditorium,
2031 Bush Street,
San Francisco, California.

Such permits will only be granted for the purpose of uniting members of a family, or in cases of grave emergency.

The Civil Control Station is equipped to assist the Japanese population affected by this evacuation in the following ways:

1. Give advice and instructions on the evacuation.

2. Provide services with respect to the management, leasing, sale, storage or other disposition of most kinds of property, such as real estate, business and professional equipment, household goods, boats, automobiles and livestock.

3. Provide temporary residence elsewhere for all Japanese in family groups.

4. Transport persons and a limited amount of clothing and equipment to their new residence.

The Following Instructions Must Be Observed:

1. A responsible member of each family, preferably the head of the family, or the person in whose name most of the property is held, and each individual living alone, will report to the Civil Control Station to receive further instructions. This must be done between 8:00 A. M. and 5:00 P. M. on Saturday, April 25, 1942, or between 8:00 A. M. and 5:00 P. M. on Sunday, April 26, 1942.

2. Evacuees must carry with them on departure for the Assembly Center, the following property:

(a) Bedding and linens (no mattress) for each member of the family;
(b) Toilet articles for each member of the family;
(c) Extra clothing for each member of the family;
(d) Sufficient knives, forks, spoons, plates, bowls and cups for each member of the family;
(e) Essential personal effects for each member of the family.

All items carried will be securely packaged, tied and plainly marked with the name of the owner and numbered in accordance with instructions obtained at the Civil Control Station.

The size and number of packages is limited to that which can be carried by the individual or family group.

3. No pets of any kind will be permitted.

4. The United States Government through its agencies will provide for the storage at the sole risk of the owner of the more substantial household items, such as iceboxes, washing machines, pianos and other heavy furniture. Cooking utensils and other small items will be accepted for storage if crated, packed and plainly marked with the name and address of the owner. Only one name and address will be used by a given family.

5. Each family, and individual living alone, will be furnished transportation to the Assembly Center or will be authorized to travel by private automobile in a supervised group. All instructions pertaining to the movement will be obtained at the Civil Control Station.

Go to the Civil Control Station between the hours of 8:00 A. M. and 5:00 P. M.,
Saturday, April 25, 1942, or between the hours of 8:00 A. M. and 5:00 P. M.,
Sunday, April 26, 1942, to receive further instructions.

J. L. DeWITT
Lieutenant General, U. S. Army
Commanding

SEE CIVILIAN EXCLUSION ORDER NO. 20.

A reminder of California's latent racial intolerance: In World War II, the entire Japanese community of 110,000 was uprooted and confined in detention camps east of the Sierra for the duration of the war—a drastic act that both the Japanese and the state would like to forget.

In search of social identity, activist spokesmen for several minorities join forces in a demonstration to secure special courses on their racial heritage at one of the state colleges.

Integration of a school district by means of school buses brings children of different racial backgrounds together in a lively, creative session in a Sausalito schoolroom. This is one of several programs throughout the state that are designed to break up segregated schools.

Self-help by Minorities

For a state that has been immeasurably enriched by the contributions of ethnic minorities, California has exhibited an unpredictable ambivalence, encouraging them on the one hand and repressing them on the other.

Historically, racial minorities have been induced to come here to build railroads, harvest crops, or work in war industries, and then, for one reason or another, some have been sent on their way or squeezed into ghettos.

Within recent years a growing pride in their racial heritage has led some of the minorities to stand up and demand a voice in their own destiny. Articulate Mexican-Americans, Negroes, California Indians, and Chinese have pressured schools, industries, housing authorities, and growers for greater recognition of their rights. Their grievances are likely to be aired for many years to come, but may well be met in California before being worked out elsewhere.

A desperate battle to save a trestle from a blazing forest is fought by a logging engine with fire-fighting attachments. Forest fires annually destroy millions of dollars of standing timber. The majority are caused by lightning, the remainder by logging operations, railroads, and campers.

Ecological Whiplash

California's ecological balance is a fragile thing, easily upset by thoughtless manipulation of the environment. In exploiting the state's resources, men have tampered with natural laws, and nature has avenged the slight. The catalogue of disaster is depressing: cities have sunk fifteen to twenty-five feet, beaches have been covered with oil slick, homes have slithered down mud slides, poor logging practices have caused forest fires and floods. Developers have been allowed to build on known earthquake faults and flood plains, and, when the once-a-generation deluge or earthquake strikes, hundreds have suffered.

Most of these blunders could have been prevented by adherence to existing codes and regulations. Some municipalities have learned their lessons painfully and well and have toughened their screening and inspection procedures. Others have not, and the list of tragic errors is likely to continue.

*Heavy downpours that strike every few years can cause mild-mannered rivers
to rise, tear out bridges, roads, rails, and homes injudiciously built in their
overflow path. Floods along the Eel (above), usually little more than an annual
nuisance, can be awesomely destructive when the drenching rainfall coincides
with heavy logging in the river's watershed.*

The unspoiled grandeur of 53,000-acre Point Reyes National Seashore was saved for the public's benefit in 1962 after a prolonged campaign by conservationists. Completion of the park is still jeopardized by plots of land within its boundaries not purchased because of insufficient appropriations.

Beauty Worth Fighting for

For more than a century, conservationists and developers have been engaged in a vendetta over California's scenic and natural wonders, but, thanks to the concerted efforts of enlightened businessmen and politicians, many of the state's natural treasures have been sequestered. Five national parks and a distinctive chain of state parks owe their existence to zealous individuals and bulldog organizations such as the Sierra Club (founded in 1892) and the Save-the-Redwoods League (founded in 1912).

Within the last few years, the drive to save the state's remaining natural wonders has resulted in the creation of two new federal parks, Point Reyes National Seashore and Redwood National Park. In the years ahead, a titanic battle yet to be fought will be the struggle to save San Francisco Bay from a host of cities and firms desiring to fill it in around its edges.

The newest area to be set aside "for the benefit and enjoyment of the people and the preservation from injury and spoliation of all timber," the Redwood National Park, dedicated in 1968, was the result of drawn-out and acrimonious negotiations involving conservationists, lumber interests, and government officials.

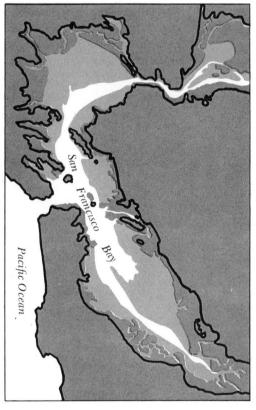

Saving San Francisco Bay from interests that are determined to fill it with a patchwork of industries and subdivisions is sure to be a struggle for years to come. The original shoreline (black line in map) encompassed a bay of seven hundred square miles. Bay lands now diked or filled have reduced the area to four hundred square miles. Potentially fillable bay lands (light gray area) would shrink the bay to a mere three hundred square miles and make it just another hot valley.

Appendix: History on the Run

It is all very well to view the history of California in the two-dimensional medium of the printed page. A reader can see the panorama of the whole state unfold before his eyes without stirring from his chair. But the person who seeks to feel and know the inner meaning of the events that created this state will doubtless wish to experience history in a third dimension and to visit the old landmarks in person.

Considering California's explosive growth, it is a wonder that there is anything left to see. Many historical landmarks have weathered away to dust; some have been submerged by urban progress, paved over with asphalt or replaced with structures to serve succeeding generations. Nevertheless, a rich collection of historical landmarks awaits the enterprising traveler, and a dozen provocative museums offer short cuts to historical artifacts.

This supplement presents a selection of the outstanding landmarks of the past that can bridge the years and speak to the citizen of today. The historical buildings and sites are grouped in these pages by eras, enabling an agile traveler to reconstitute a particular period by visiting the surviving mementos that best represent it.

In addition, as an aid to assist the reader in choosing what to see first, the historical places have been keyed with symbols that rate their relative appeal. By means of this ranking scheme, a visitor can choose which places are worth his time and interest and can schedule accordingly.

KEY TO RATING CODE

All points listed in this appendix are historically important, but some are more revealing than others. Ratings in this guide are arbitrary judgments by the author—with a half-dozen experts whispering in his ear.

**** A place that communicates the atmosphere of its era with special cogency. Well worth a trip as well as a half to a full day's visit.

*** Worth a trip even though the landmark may represent only one facet of the life of its time. A visit can absorb up to a half day's time.

** Worth an hour's visit if you are nearby.

* Historically important but visually so-so.

(No symbol.) Historically important but only as a site. Nothing there to see.

Legend and Lure, 1540–1769

Explorers from New Spain left few traces of their visits to the land now known as California. Beyond a spate of melodious place names, some shards of chinaware from ships wrecked on the rocky headlands, and one brass plate, nothing tangible was left behind.

All one can do today is to read the explorers' journals, then visit the ancient landing places and compare the way they look today with how they were described four centuries ago.

FORT YUMA, Imperial County. Probable site of the first European footprints in California. In 1540 a party under Hernando de Alarcón is presumed to have stepped ashore here from boats while exploring the Colorado River delta. This group was followed the same year by Melchior Dior, who was sent to rendezvous with Alarcón, missed him, and returned to New Spain.

*** CABRILLO NATIONAL MONUMENT, Point Loma, San Diego. Within this compound or nearby are a number of important Spanish sites. Here Juan Cabrillo landed (1542), Sebastián Vizcaíno built a temporary house of prayer (1602), the first Spanish graves were dug (1769), the first coastal beacon lighted, and a shore battery installed (1797–1800). Museum and lighthouse (1855).

** VIZCAINO LANDING (1603), Monterey, Pacific Street near Presidio gate. It was here that Vizcaíno became enamored of Monterey Bay, "the noble harbor, sheltered from all winds." Site only.

** DRAKES BAY, off Highway 1, sixty miles north of San Francisco. Fine rugged landing site where Drake careened his vessel in 1579 and remained for six weeks. A brass plate, left by the expedition, was found 357 years later and is now displayed in the BANCROFT LIBRARY, University of California, Berkeley. Drakes Bay was also the setting for the wreck of a Manila galleon, captained by Sebastián Cermeño, in 1595. Cermeño returned to New Spain in a small launch. Neither party sighted San Francisco Bay. Small museum.

Indian Eden, 30,000 B.C.–1769

Only the most fragmentary relics are left from the Indians' millennial occupation of California. An occasional shell mound may still be visible, particularly in the San Francisco Bay area. Rock paintings exist alongside ancient Indian trails in the back country, pock-marked rocks are scattered throughout the oak region where Indian women once ground acorns, and obsidian arrowheads and chips are churned up by plows, bulldozers—and sharp-eyed children—in many parts of the state. Otherwise, little remains of a rich culture swept under by two alien civilizations. Indian artifacts were destroyed or scattered; fortunately, some have been sequestered in museums.

*** STATE INDIAN MUSEUM, Sacramento. Fine collection of California Indian handicrafts: baskets, pottery, weapons, boats, clothing. The museum seems somewhat antiquated by modern standards, but it does contain a rich treasure, clearly labeled and displayed in no-nonsense fashion.

** OAKLAND MUSEUM, 1000 Fallon Street, Oakland. Modern presentation of California Indian culture.

* LOWIE MUSEUM OF ANTHROPOLOGY, University of California, Berkeley. Produces occasional exhibits stocked from the university's vast collection of Indian artifacts. Museum is small and select.

** SANTA BARBARA MUSEUM OF NATURAL HISTORY, 2559 Puesta del Sol Road, Santa Barbara. Fine collection of materials related to the Channel Indians, a highly advanced tribal group.

** LOS ANGELES COUNTY MUSEUM OF NATURAL HISTORY, Exposition Park, Los Angeles. Good collection of dioramas, models, and artifacts.

*** SOUTHWEST MUSEUM, 234 Museum Drive, Highland Park. Specializes in the Indians of the Southwest but maintains a good display of California Indian artifacts. An intimate and musty museum, dating from the 1920's, but one of the best in the nation.

** MUSEUM OF MAN, Balboa Park, San Diego. Fine exhibits on California Indians related to story of man in North, Central and South America.

* MALKI MUSEUM, Banning, and * AMERICAN INDIAN HISTORICAL SOCIETY MUSEUM, San Francisco, are the only museums in the state maintained by California Indians. Other museums are located in most of the county seats.

Spanish Transplant, 1769–1822

Remnants of the Spanish colonization abound, principally in the form of mission chapels, restored with varying degrees of completeness and authenticity over the last century. Most of the buildings were left to the mercy of weather and vandals after secularization, and when restoration began in the 1870's, many of them had almost vanished. What is popularly known as a California mission today is in most cases simply the chapel, which was only one feature of the mission complex.

Restoration of presidios and pueblos has not attracted much support, and the remnants of these institutions are fragmentary at best.

** MISSION SAN DIEGO (1769), on Mission Valley Road, off Interstate 8. Historically important as the first mission in Alta California, but the church building, which originally dates from the 1820's, has been indifferently restored and furnished. Touristy.

* PRESIDIO OF SAN DIEGO (1769), on Presidio Drive. Site. Not much to see. Archaeological excavations in progress.

*** MISSION SAN LUIS REY (1797), on Highway 76. Once a wide-spreading mission compound, it has been only partly restored. Unusual chapel; pleasant gardens.

*** MISSION SAN JUAN CAPISTRANO (1776), on Interstate 5. A tourist trap, but a fascinating place. Scene of the televised return of the swallows on or about St. Joseph's Day, March 19.

** PUEBLO DE LOS ANGELES STATE HISTORICAL MONUMENT, near Los Angeles Civic Center. Includes SITE OF THE PUEBLO OF LOS ANGELES (1781), marked by a bronze plaque and statue of the governor who established the second of California's three pueblos. Nearby stands Los Angeles' oldest building, the AVILA ADOBE (1818), a portion of a once-imposing town house, now serving as a museum. On the Plaza is the PLAZA CHURCH (1822), a grossly modernized chapel where all of Los Angeles once worshiped.

** MISSION SAN GABRIEL (1771), on Mission Drive, ten miles east of Los Angeles. Only the chapel remains of what was once one of the most extensive mission developments. On display a remarkable set of paintings of the Stations of the Cross by a mission Indian.

*** MISSION SAN FERNANDO (1797), 15151 San Fernando Mission Boulevard. Excellently restored Convento—the largest adobe building in the mission chain. Fine museum and gardens.

** MISSION SAN BUENAVENTURA (1782), Main and Figueroa streets, Ventura. Well-preserved sanctuary with good collection of mission relics. Museum.

**** MISSION SANTA BARBARA (1786), State and Laguna streets, Santa Barbara. Imposing architectural union of Greek and Moorish motifs. Museum.

*** MISSION SANTA INES (1804), Solvang. Fine collection of vestments, paintings, and antiquities. Unusual wall behind the altar.

**** MISSION LA PURISMA CONCEPCION (1787), west of intersection of US 101 and Buellton. Com-

plete and authentic restoration of an entire mission compound by the state. The only one of the missions that shows the full scope of mission activities. Crammed with exhibits. Even the garden is authentic.

** MISSION SAN LUIS OBISPO (1772), Monterey and Chorro streets, San Luis Obispo. Reasonably accurate restoration of a much-remodeled church. Museum.

** MISSION SAN MIGUEL ARCANGEL (1797), just off US 101 in San Miguel. Fairly intact church and some of the attached structure. Remarkable altar wall and quaint pulpit. Features seasonal fiestas.

*** MISSION SAN ANTONIO DE PADUA (1771), on side road twenty-five miles west of King City. Mission was reconstructed from the ground up in the 1950's. Museum and seasonal festivals.

* MISSION SOLEDAD (1791), one mile west of US 101, three miles south of town of Soledad. A modest but conscientious reconstruction. Small museum.

**** MISSION SAN CARLOS BORROMEO (1770), Carmel. Former headquarters of the mission chain and a romantic old stone building, crammed with venerable and authentic relics. Burial site of Father Junípero Serra and his successor, Father Fermín Lasuén, presidents of the California missions.

** ROYAL PRESIDIO CHAPEL (1795), Church Street, Monterey. Nearly intact, the only Spanish presidio chapel remaining in the state. Present stone building replaced original structure built in 1770.

* MISSION SANTA CRUZ (1791), Emmet and School streets, Santa Cruz. Two-thirds scale reproduction of mission chapel that had crumbled into dust. Tiny museum.

*** MISSION SAN JUAN BAUTISTA, in San Juan, off US 101. Large, relatively intact church with interesting altar wall. Museum. Mission fronts on plaza of SAN JUAN BAUTISTA STATE HISTORIC PARK, an engaging re-creation of a California town of the 1850's.

* MISSION SANTA CLARA (1777), University of Santa Clara. Modern reconstruction of a building destroyed by fire in 1929. Interesting ceiling painting, copied from one in the original structure. Good museum.

* MISSION SAN JOSE (1791), on Highway 21. Small fragment of original structure, now a museum. Set in midst of eighteenth-century olive grove.

*** MISSION DOLORES (1776), Sixteenth and Dolores streets, San Francisco. Original chapel is all that remains of mission. Relatively intact, fine, musty old building. Fascinating cemetery harbors the remains of some of the illustrious and notorious characters of early San Francisco.

* PRESIDIO OF SAN FRANCISCO (1776), Lombard and Lyon streets. Commanding site of Spanish garrison. Some sixteenth-century cannon cast in Peru and a very modernized adobe, now used in the officers' club, comprise the sole mementos. Shore battery site (1794) located where Fort Winfield Scott now stands.

*** FORT ROSS (1812), ninety miles north of San Francisco on Highway 1. Redwood fortress built by Russians in casual defiance of the Spaniards. Occupied for thirty-one years. Meticulously restored by the state, the fort has many interesting exhibits.

Restless Arcadia, 1822–46

Surviving mementos of the two decades of Mexican rule reflect the change from a church-dominated society to a landowning aristocracy based on cattle ranching. Trade with the outside world brought money and amenities to the province, permitting the building and furnishing of comfortable adobe homes. Many of these are still standing, in varying degrees of preservation, and a few are well worth a visit for their gracious atmosphere. These are the homes that served as the prototypes for the Spanish ranch houses that proliferated in the 1950's.

*** OLD TOWN, SAN DIEGO (1820's). A cluster of pleasant adobe homes remains from the area that was the center of town during the Mexican period. Best known is Ramona's Marriage Place (a delightful hoax, since Ramona existed only in the imagination of author Helen Hunt Jackson), stocked with antiquities of considerable interest. The somnolent PLAZA was once the setting for bullfights and fiestas.

HIDE PARK (1824–46), La Playa, San Diego. Site of cosmopolitan colony of hide droghers established by Boston trading ships. Colony once had eight hundred men working on hide processing. First raising of U.S. flag occurred informally here in 1829. Described by Richard Henry Dana in *Two Years Before the Mast*.

*** HUGO REID ADOBE (1839), Los Angeles State and County Arboretum, Arcadia. Beautifully furnished, restored adobe, once headquarters for thirteen-thousand-acre Rancho Santa Anita.

** LOS CERRITOS ADOBE (1837), 4600 Virginia Road, Long Beach. Large, well-furnished ranch home.

*** EL PUEBLO VIEJO, Santa Barbara. This 16-block historic reservation in the center of the city, has a number of authentic adobes, dating from 1820–40, identified on a "path of history." Most interesting is the CASA DE LA GUERRA (1819–26), originally built by the commandant of the presidio of Santa Barbara. It was described by Richard Henry Dana in *Two Years Before the Mast*. Presently devoted to craft shops.

**** MONTEREY PATH OF HISTORY, a self-guided tour of the score of adobes dating from Monterey's decades as the provincial capital. Because this city was bypassed by history after the American take-over, many of its original adobes were undisturbed by the urban growth that destroyed Mexican homes in other cities. Few of these buildings were occupied by Makers of History, but they have been lovingly restored and they exude atmosphere. Several fine museums in the city.

MISSION SAN RAFAEL ARCANGEL (1817), Fifth Avenue and A Street, San Rafael. No one really knows what this mission looked like, because it disintegrated soon after secularization. No sketches survive of the building while it was in use. Design of the present structure (built in 1949) is pure guesswork. The mission served as a hospital for sick Indians from Mission Dolores in San Francisco.

** PETALUMA ADOBE (1834), four miles east of Petaluma. Built by Indian labor for General Mariano Vallejo over a ten-year period, this enormous adobe was the headquarters for the general's extensive ranch operations. The building has been meticulously restored by the state and outfitted with meaningful exhibits.

*** SONOMA STATE HISTORIC PARK, on Highway 12. Restored remnants of the settlement founded in 1834 by General Vallejo as a bastion against the Russians to the north. Buildings are grouped around a plaza where the Mexican troops drilled. The adobe BARRACKS (1837) were the headquarters of the Bear Flag Revolt, which erupted here in 1846. Vallejo was taken captive here by the insurgents and imprisoned at Sutter's Fort for two months. MISSION SAN FRANCISCO SOLANO (1823), the last of the Franciscan missions, was founded as a threat to the Russians. Now a state-owned museum,

it is sparsely equipped but has an outstanding series of water-color paintings of the missions.

**** SUTTER'S FORT (1839), Sacramento. Trading center, military outpost, and ranch headquarters for the industrious and visionary John A. Sutter, who dreamed of establishing a state-within-a-state. The fort became a rallying point for the first American settlers in Mexican California. Fully restored, with reasonable accuracy, it contains numerous exhibits of craft shops, living quarters, and pioneer relics that span several decades of history.

Yankee Take-over, 1846–47

The six months' war between the Californios and the United States was too brief, too fluid, and involved too few participants to leave behind any of the traditional battlefield memorabilia. Bronze tablets mark the sites of the few skirmishes that were fought, memorialize every house and hovel that sheltered John Charles Frémont in his wanderings, and identify every hacienda that served as headquarters for Commodore Stockton, Lieutenant William Tecumseh Sherman, and other military luminaries.

The war started in the north and moved south. Dedicated followers of military history may well enjoy reliving this brief campaign by visiting these sites:

Bear Flag Revolt

*** SONOMA STATE HISTORIC PARK, on Highway 12. The Bear Flag was raised here in the plaza June 14, 1846, and prominent Californios taken prisoner. The flag was replaced July 9 by the Stars and Stripes, raised by the grandson of Paul Revere.

**** SUTTER'S FORT, Sacramento. General Vallejo was kept prisoner here for two months by the insurgents.

* SOCIETY OF CALIFORNIA PIONEERS MUSEUM, San Francisco, has many memorabilia of the Bear Flaggers.

Military Occupation of Northern California

*** MEXICAN CUSTOM HOUSE (1827), Monterey. American flag was first raised here by United States forces on July 7, 1846. (Also raised here by mistake four years earlier.) Building contains a state-operated museum with first-class exhibits on Monterey history.

*** LARKIN HOUSE (1835), Monterey. Home of Thomas O. Larkin, the key figure in the conspiracy to acquire California by peaceful annexation. A beguiling house, prototype of the Monterey colonial residential architecture, it is inappropriately furnished with antiques of a later period than Larkin's occupancy.

FREMONT PEAK, Fremont Peak State Park, near San Juan. Site of Frémont's belligerent threat to the Californios in March 1846. With a small band, Frémont built a log fort and flew the American flag over it for four days before retreating before a company of Californios assembled to dislodge him. Episode caused mistrust on both sides, is regarded as a cause of the Bear Flag Revolt.

BATTLE OF NATIVIDAD, on side road 6.7 miles east of Salinas. Site of the only battle in Northern California, fought November 16, 1846, between a party of California lancers and American irregulars. Score: four dead and four wounded Americans and an equal number of casualties among the Californios.

Military Occupation of Southern California

Bronze tablets mark the sites of skirmishes, headquarters of the combatants, and innumerable flag raisings in Los Angeles, San Diego, and Santa Barbara.

** SAN PASQUAL BATTLEFIELD, seven miles east of Escondido. Weed-grown, arid setting for the bloody defeat of the Army of the West by California lancers December 6, 1846. The twenty-one American cavalrymen killed in this encounter are interred in Fort Rosecrans National Cemetery on Point Loma, San Diego.

SITE OF FORT MOORE (1847), near Los Angeles Civic Center. Marked by a monumental bas-relief, this eminence was occupied off and on by United States troops during the subduing of rebellious Los Angeles. American forces were driven from this post in September 1846 and prevented from returning until January.

* SITE OF SIGNING OF CAPITULATION, 3919 Lankershim Boulevard, North Hollywood. Here Andrés Pico and John C. Frémont signed the treaty that ended the war in California, January 13, 1847.

Rush for Gold, 1849–54

In the brief span of five years, the Gold Rush transformed the northern part of the state, created a string of mining towns in foothill country that had once belonged only to the Indians—and then evaporated. The deflation was almost as rapid as the explosive build-up of the Gold Rush. Left behind in the collapse were dozens of ghost towns, quantities of rusting mining machinery, and a score of vigorous settlements that have stubbornly survived to this day. A trip along the twisting length of State Highway 49 takes the visitor through towns that are subsisting on legend, some that have exploited the past with neon honky-tonk, and some that have developed substantial interests no longer connected with the gold fever.

**** COLUMBIA HISTORIC STATE PARK (1850), on Highway 49. A conscientious re-creation of a gold town of the 1850's, Columbia exudes atmosphere, some of it authentic, some of it good-humoredly phony. A participants' town, it features restaurants, stores, bars, and candy manufacturers where the wares of yesterday can be obtained in colorful surroundings. One of the few places in the state where one can ride in a Concord stage.

* COLOMA, on Highway 49. Site of Marshall's gold discovery in January 1848.

** NEVADA CITY, on Highway 49. Least spoiled of the gold towns. Excellent museum.

** ANGELS CAMP, on Highway 49. Modernized but the setting for the annual Jumping Frog Jubilee in May.

Other Gold Rush towns worth a visit: VOLCANO, MURPHYS, MOKELUMNE HILL, JACKSON.

**** SUTTER'S FORT, Sacramento. Loaded with Gold Rush knickknacks and mining paraphernalia.

* OLD SACRAMENTO, a few blocks of the old river front have been set aside as a historic park. Run down and propped up, the area awaits appropriation of funds for complete development.

*** MALAKOFF DIGGINGS, on the road to North Bloomfield. An extraordinary sight, man-made wasteland created by hydraulic monitors in the 1860's.

SAN FRANCISCO, though the major port of entry for the gold seekers, lost most of its Gold Rush relics to make room for more modern buildings in the first years of pell-mell growth and lost the rest in the fire of 1906. Bronze plaques mark many of the important sites and outline the original shoreline that once ran where the financial district now stands. Two good museums display a number of selected artifacts.

*** WELLS FARGO BANK HISTORY ROOM, 420 Montgomery Street. A remarkable, compact exhibit of Gold Rush materials. Friendly and informed attendants dispense information at the drop of a question mark.

** SOCIETY OF CALIFORNIA PIONEERS, 46 McAllister Street. A selective display of antiquities.

Raw Young State, 1850–70

The mushrooming new state outpaced its governmental institutions and surged ahead without control on several fronts. With exuberant faith in the inexhaustibility of the state's resources, the newcomers felled forests, dammed rivers, and exploited scenic wonders. In the absence of legal machinery, they improvised their own hemp justice, and the state is sprinkled with bronze tablets recording lynchings, riots, duels, and assassinations. Alongside these nefarious doings, solid growth produced a number of substantial buildings, parks, and harbor developments that are still visible.

Some of the first STATE CAPITOLS are still on view. ** COLTON HALL, Monterey, was the setting for the state's constitutional convention in 1847. An austere building, it contains a modest museum. SITE OF FIRST CAPITOL, SAN JOSE, 100 block of South Market Street. SITE OF SECOND CAPITOL, VALLEJO, 215–19 York Street. * THIRD CAPITOL, BENICIA, First and G streets. Immaculately restored building that housed the legislature, 1853–54.

*** STATE CAPITOL, SACRAMENTO, Capitol Park. Built soon after the legislature moved from Benicia, the classic-style building was patterned after the national capitol. The building is burdened with a variety of exhibits of uneven quality and interest relating to the history of the state since 1850. Capitol Park contains trees from every state.

** LOS ANGELES PUEBLO STATE HISTORICAL MONUMENT, near the Civic Center in downtown Los Angeles. Though starved for funds, the old plaza area is being slowly restored to approximate its status in the 1860's. A firehouse, hotel, stores, and a theater make up the complex, which will be completed when necessary funds are provided. OLVERA STREET, which runs off the plaza area, is a later development. The remnants of the old Cow Town have long ago been razed for parking lots or additions to the Civic Center.

*** PIONEER VILLAGE, Bakersfield, 3801 Chester Avenue. A conscientious project to reconstitute the early days of the southern end of the Central Valley, consists of old structures disassembled and rebuilt in a twelve-acre park. A school, general store, homes, and an oil derrick are among the main attractions.

*** CONVERSE BASIN, General Grant Grove, Kings Canyon National Park. High up in the Sierra, a wasteland of gigantic stumps was left behind by loggers who stripped the big trees off the land in the 1860's and 1870's before governmental controls could stop them. Ancient sawdust piles are still fresh after nearly a century.

***CAPTAIN JACK'S STRONGHOLD, Lava Beds National Monument, on Highway 139. Scene of the last outbreak of Indian hostility in the 1870's. Band of 150 Modoc Indians held off a large force of United States troops for several months in a bloody siege. Jumbled terrain provided natural cover for the Indians.

End of Insularity, 1852–69

Progressive improvement in the modes of transportation that characterized the latter half of the nineteenth century helped to break down California's long isolation and bring the state into intimate contact with the outside world. Some of the ships, stagecoaches, and trains that helped break California's long sleep are displayed in several collections.

Ships

***SAN FRANCISCO MARITIME MUSEUM, foot of Hyde Street. Outstanding museum devoted to Pacific maritime commerce. Models, diagrams, maps, dioramas, and nautical gear fill a bay-side museum. Nearby are the restored hulls of a dozen types of sailing and steam vessels that opened California to the Orient and the world. Best known: the **BALCLUTHA (1886), a steel-hulled lime-juicer that served for many years in the Alaskan salmon fishery.

**CABRILLO BEACH MARINE MUSEUM, 3720 Stephen White Drive, San Pedro. A crowded little museum with every square inch filled with maritime gear, models, and old photographs. Fine collection of seashells.

***STAR OF INDIA, San Diego Harbor. Twin of the *Balclutha,* hundred-year-old, iron-hulled ship built in Glasgow.

Stagecoaching and Pony Express

***WELLS FARGO BANK HISTORY ROOM, 420 Montgomery Street, San Francisco. Plenty of lore on the stagecoaches that served the West and have become the trademark of the Wells Fargo Bank. Resplendent Concord coach nearly fills the compact museum.

CONCORD STAGECOACHES are also displayed in Yreka, Sutter's Fort, Sacramento; Columbia (available for rides); Society of California Pioneers, San Francisco; Los Angeles County Museum of Natural Sciences, Exposition Park, Los Angeles; and Serra Museum, San Diego.

Stage stations are a dime a dozen throughout the state.

Railroadiana

***TRAVEL TOWN, Griffith Park, Los Angeles. The best assemblage of rolling stock in the state, this collection of ancient locomotives, passenger cars, gondolas, and streetcars is open for the most personal inspection. A great clambering spot for small boys.

Live steamers still pull vintage trains over short lines in a few localities. Best known is the SUPER-SKUNK that runs for 40 miles along the Noyo River between Fort Bragg and Willits. Touristy but good clean nostalgia. Another popular run in the Santa Cruz Mountains is the vintage ROARING CAMP AND BIG TREES NARROW-GAUGE RAILROAD that runs through five miles of redwood forest.

When it is completed, the railroad exhibit in OLD SACRAMENTO promises to be an outstanding display of sedentary and rolling railroad equipment. Plans call for a tie-in with resurrected river boats for train-boat excursions.

Boomland, 1880–90

Physical remnants from the period of the Great Boom in Southern California are as evanescent as the boom itself. Still standing are a few ivy-encrusted college buildings dating from the peak of the real estate extravaganza and a few venerable resort hotels; but gone is the web of streetcar lines that once linked the boom towns together; gone too are the flashier developments, such as Coronado's tent city and incredible Venice, with its canals, Italian architecture, and singing gondoliers.

Evidence of the great citrus and oil booms can be seen on the outskirts of Los Angeles. It is still possible to drive for miles through groves of fragrant orange trees, set out by the thousands in the 1880's east of Los Angeles. One may also make a less appealing excursion through the stark forests of oil derricks, planted on the hills and mountains surrounding Los Angeles. There is only one place where one can find a distillate of the great oil boom that shaped the economic destiny of Southern California, and that is the OIL MUSEUM in Santa Paula, maintained by the Union Oil Company.

One lone survivor from the era of the great resorts is well worth a visit:

***HOTEL DEL CORONADO (1888), Coronado. This extraordinary architectural confection, built on a sandy wasteland at the peak of the boom, epitomizes the boundless optimism of the 1880's. Still one of the country's notable hotels.

New Century, New Order, 1900–30

Developments since 1900 are still too recent to inspire the protective instincts of antiquarians.

Oddly enough, the motion picture industry, seemingly the best candidate for encasing in museum amber, is meagerly represented. A small museum in Hollywood, *LYTTON CENTER OF THE VISUAL ARTS, 8150 Sunset Boulevard, displays some early-early paraphernalia, but a first-rate assemblage of historical material for public viewing is still to be developed. The usual bronze tablets and a quirky monument or two are all that remind the public that a great industry started here in 1910.

***UNIVERSAL CITY STUDIOS, 3900 Lankersheim Boulevard, Universal City. Although this studio contains some oldish sets, it represents largely a cross section of the industry after 1940. A fascinating inside look.

The early days of the airplane industry are likewise neglected. The best collection of vintage aircraft is displayed at the **AIR MUSEUM, at Ontario, but few of the craft were manufactured in the state. The display, however, includes planes that are contemporaries of those glued together here in the early decades of this century.

Two international expositions that celebrated completion of the Panama Canal have left behind some significant relics:

***SAN DIEGO EXPOSITION GROUNDS (1915–16), Balboa Park. Some of the richly ornamented buildings, created for the jewel-like exposition, have been restored and are still in use. Most notable survivor is the handsome California Tower complex, constructed of permanent materials. The architectural style of this exposition exerted a lasting influence over the design of public buildings in California.

**PALACE OF FINE ARTS (1915), San Francisco, is the sole accessible remnant of the plaster-and-chicken-wire structures of the Panama-Pacific International Exposition, a romantic splurge that drew two million visitors to its exhibits from twenty-five countries.

Acknowledgments

Grateful acknowledgment is made to the many friends who helped in the assembling and checking of material for this book. In addition to those mentioned in the Foreword, I would like to give special thanks to Raymond Aker of the Drake Navigators Guild for drawings and counsel for the opening chapter; to Dr. Albert B. Elsasser, of the Lowie Museum of Anthropology, for guidance on the Indian material; to Harry Downie, redoubtable restorer of missions, for help on the Spanish interlude; to Allan R. Ottley and his staff of the California Room of the State Library for tips on little-used materials; to George Kraus, of the Southern Pacific, for railroadiana; to Albert M. Harmon and Matilda Dring, of the San Francisco Maritime Museum, for maritime graphics; to Irene Simpson Neasham and her comely crew at the Wells Fargo Bank History Room, San Francisco, and to Larry Booth, of San Diego's Title Insurance and Trust Company, for a photographic bonanza.

For diverse favors, the author also wishes to thank Kramer Adams, Dr. Joseph Baird, William Bronson, Richard Dillon, Newton B. Drury, Donald Duke, Dr. Eliot Evans, Helen Giffen, Ralph Hansen, Walter Houk, John Hussey, Joseph LeBarbara, Hank Johnston, Jerry MacMullen, W. W. Robinson, Waddell Smith, and Shirley Sargent.

Picture Credits

(Key: t—top, b—bottom, c—center, l—left, r—right)

Index